STORIES FROM THE CELL

Fifty Margaret River Wineries Tell Their Tales

Jane Scott   Patricia Negus

CAPE TO CAPE PUBLISHING

First published October 2011
Copyright © Patricia Negus and Jane Scott, 2011

National Library of Australia Cataloguing-in-Publication entry

Author: Scott, Jane.

Title: Stories from the cellar door : fifty Margaret River wineries tell their tales / Jane Scott Patricia Negus.

ISBN: 9780980333763 (pbk.)

Subjects: Wineries–Western Australia–Margaret River Region.
               Wine and wine making–Western Australia–Margaret River Region.
               Wine districts–Western Australia–Margaret River Region.
               Margaret River Region (W.A.)–Description and travel.
               Margaret River Region (W.A.)–Guidebooks.
               Margaret River Region (W.A.)–History.

Other Authors/Contributors: Negus, Patricia.

Dewey Number: 641.22099412

Front cover: The Geese at Cape Mentelle; Inside front and back cover main photos by Miranda Quenby.
Photos: Jane Scott, Patricia Negus, Ray Forma
Produced and Printed entirely in Australia.
Cape to Cape Publishing, 50 Harvest Road, North Fremantle WA 6159, Australia
http://capetocape.8m.com & capetocape@smartchat.net.au
Production & typesetting: Ray Forma
Typeset in 10 pt Times and Helvetica
Please let us know about updates, corrections, suggestions and improvements at capetocape@smartchat.net.au.
Updates and corrections are available at http://capetocape.8m.com or by scanning the following QR code:

Prepress and Printing in Western Australia by

To produce this book Scott Print used vegetable-based inks on paper that is chlorine-free and made from plantation grown timber. Both the paper manufacturer and the printer are certified to the highest internationally-recognised standard for environmental management.

Introduction

Previous publications from Cape to Cape Publishing have been about natural history – wildflowers, fungi, birds, fish, shells – and guidebooks to walks in the south west corner of Western Australia. In this book, we have focused on a different subject altogether, on the stories behind some of Margaret River's wineries and their people.

As our project evolved, we have met many fabulous people and heard some fascinating stories about the making of individual wineries, about what went before, about their owners' histories, and about some of the funny incidents that have happened along the way. We have woven into these some of the history of the region and of the Margaret River wine industry. Some snippets of geography and flora and fauna facts have also found their way into our book.

Every story is unique, but common threads emerged as we gathered information. There were the hardships and struggles faced by the pioneers of an industry that had an uncertain future, the ravages of young vines by marauding cattle and of grapes by silvereyes, and the journey into the unknown by so many who had left previous professions and walks of life for one about which they knew very little. For some it was the lure of the beautiful countryside of Australia's south west corner, for some a lifestyle change or a retirement project, for some just the love of good wine, but invariably the romantic ideal quickly turned into the reality of hard work! In all the stories that we heard there was a uniting theme: the passions and aspirations of the people that we met to make great wines in one of the best grape-growing areas in the world.

The stories are brought alive with Patricia's delightful paintings.

Our goal was 50 wineries, with the criteria that they had to have a story to tell, and something unique that Patricia could paint. There are others we could have included, but if this book was to see the light of day we needed to set a limit. There is always the prospect of a second edition!

Acknowledgements

In addition to all the current winery owners and staff, who have been tremendously helpful and positive towards our project, we would like to thank the following: Jeff Gallagher, David Gregg, Gail Varis, Ross Woodhouse, Bobbie Drew, Conor Lagan, John Yates, John Alferink, John Williams, Keith Lightbody, Phil Paine, Rosmarie Thomson, Sue Graham-Taylor, Andrea and Eion Lindsay, Ian Rooke, the West family, Kelly Gherardi, Bridget Haak, Giles Hohnen, Molly Hall, Miranda Quenby & Roger Scott.

MAP & CONTENTS

After each winery is the page number
on which that winery's description starts.

Cape Naturaliste

Bunker Bay

Eagle Bay

Meelup

Sugarloaf

Castle Bay

Geographe Bay

Wise Wines p98

Indian Ocean

Dunsborough

Caves Road

Ngilgi Cave

Yallingup

Caves Road

Busselton Bypass

Cape Naturaliste Vineyard p28

Smiths Beach

Vasse

Bussell Highway

Lamonts p60
Koorabin Dr
Marrinup Dr

Happs Vineyard p46

Carbunup

Canal Rocks →

Marri Wood Park p68
Whittle Rd
Wyadup

Wildwood Road

Caves Road

Injidup

Cape Clairault

Aravina p10

Anniebrook p8

Abbey Farm Rd

Yelverton Rd Nth

North Jindong Rd

Clairault p32

Henry Rd

Yelverton Rd

Roy Road

Payne Road (to Busselton)

Laurance p62

Johnson Rd

Pusey Road

Willespie p96
Woody Nook p102

Island Brook p56

Saracen p84

Moses Rock Rd

Rosily p82

Flying Fish p40

Knotting Hill p58
The Grove P88
Carter Rd

Churchview Estate p30
Gale Road
Metricup Road
Harmans Mill Rd

Lenton Brae p66

Woodlands p100

Pierro p76

Brookland Valley p18

Gralyn p42

Hay Shed Hill p48

Jindong Treeton Rd

Cullen p34

Howling Wolves p54
Tom Cullity Drive
Heydon Estate p50
Bettenay p14
Miamup Rd

Vasse Felix p90

Brockman Rd

Howard Park p52

Treeton Road Nth

Key

— Sealed Road

Gravel Road

Leeuwin-Naturaliste National Park

Cape to Cape Track

Treeton Road

Cape Grace p24

Fifty One Rd

Cowaramup

Brookwood Estate p20

Cowaramup Bay

Gracetown

Caves Road

Cowaramup Bay Rd

Ellen Brook Rd

Adinfern p6

Edwards p36

Burnside Rd

Osmington Road

Ellensbrook

Carters Road

Rosa Brook

Rosa Brook Rd (to Sues Rd)

McHenry Hohnen Vintners p70

Xanadu p104
Wallcliffe Road
Cape Mentelle p26

Margaret River

Brown Hill p22

Darch Road

Rosa Brook Rd

Rosa Glen Rd

Preveli Wines p78
Mitchell Drive

Minot p74

Watershed p94

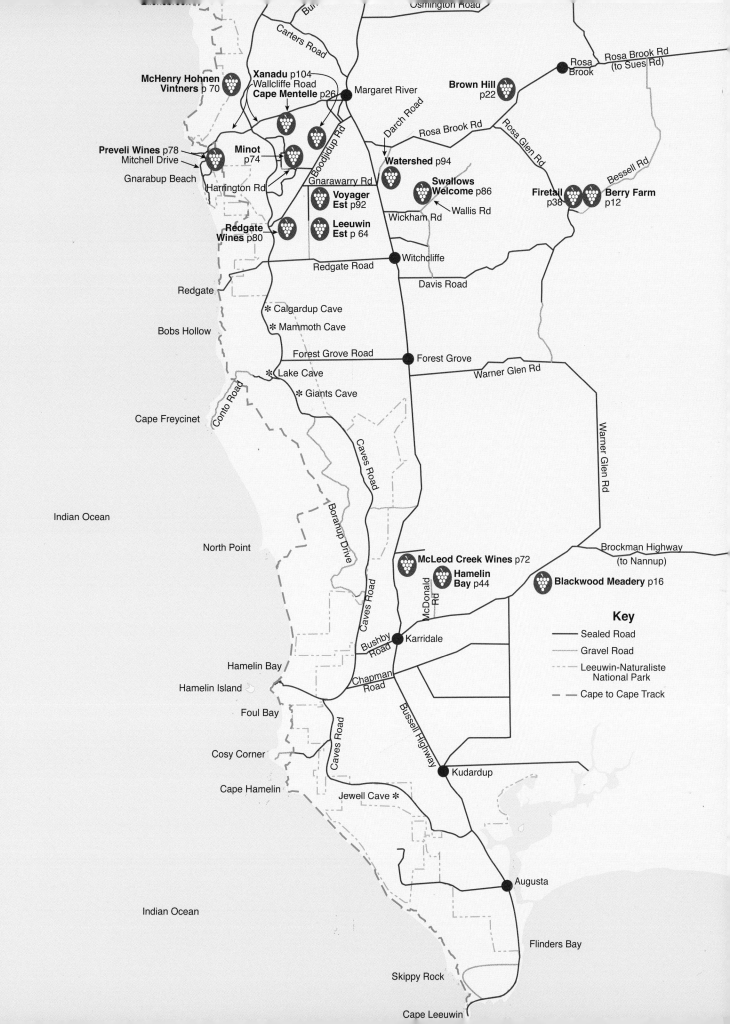

ADINFERN ESTATE

Established: 1996

Merv Smith of Adinfern Estate has seen a few changes since moving to the farm in the 1950s with parents, Don and Betty, when he was five years old. Margaret River was then a sleepy little post-war town in a rather depressed rural district, and the reaction from their friends and neighbours in Harvey was "Why would you want to go there?"

Merv's parents built up a dairy farm, but changed to sheep in 1969 when wool prices were at a premium. After growing up fishing on the coast and catching gilgies in the streams, Merv travelled around the state as a shearer before returning to Margaret River to take over the farm with new wife, Jan, in 1972. This was the era when surfers from Perth and the Eastern States were beginning to discover the awesome Margaret River waves. Jan was one of the first female tellers for the Bank of New South Wales to 'go bush' from Perth, and she remembers the novelty of stamping the pass books of clients at the Margaret River branch who had come all the way from Sydney! These were the days when even a visitor from Bunbury caused a great stir in the town.

With falling wool prices, but with tourism in the area on the rise, the Smiths augmented their income by opening the farm to the public, and holding shearing demonstrations, quite a logistical exercise, with small batches of sheep needing to be ready for shearing any day of the year. Besides the sheep, there were goats, cows and chickens to feed, and the farm was especially popular with school groups. It was around this time that Merv, now no spring chicken himself, set to accomplish his record quota of 202 sheep in a day. He felt that he should try to match the young blokes he was teaching, as they could all shear this many without any trouble – obviously he was a good teacher!

But even at 40, Merv was saying he didn't know what he wanted to do when he grew up, and after the crash in wool prices in 1989, which didn't improve over the next few years, he and Jan finally decided to change tack completely, and they began to plant their vineyard in 1996. At the age of 50, along with several other Margaret River 'oldies', including Tim Negus of Swallows Welcome, Merv went back to school to take the TAFE course in viticulture. Adinfern Estate started off with a modest 15 acres of vines, expanding gradually to the current 70 acres. They are still very much a family operation however, with Jan, Merv and son Ian working the vineyard, making and marketing their wines and running the cellar door. And in the best family tradition, they nurture their pickers and pruners, many of whom are drawn from the pool of young backpackers who come to work in the region from all over the world.

The blade shears below went out of use in the 1900s. In 1892 Jackie Howe set the record for shearing 321 sheep in one day. They are still in use in cold climates because they don't cut so close to the sheep's skin.

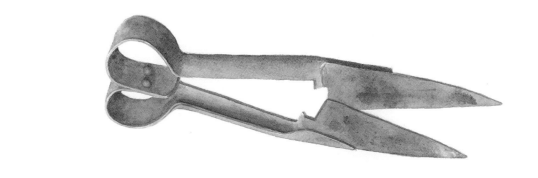

From Wool to Wine

ANNIEBROOK

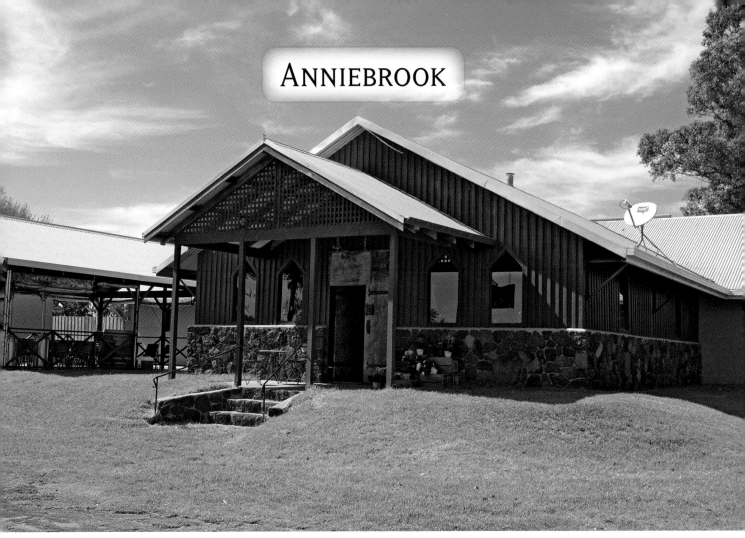

Established: 1986

After the First World War, there was a major surge in population to the South West of Western Australia, as people were encouraged to emigrate from Britain to the portrayed pristine lands of the new colony. Mostly, this flood of people came with the Group Settlement Scheme (see Churchview), but there were also a number of soldiers who were resettled in Western Australia after the War, and given land as a reward for service. One of these was Harry Lewis, who had been an artillery horseman, and had decided, when it was all over, that his best chance for the future was to take up land in Australia's South West.

Sixty years on, third generation farmers Wally and Dawn Lewis completed what Harry had started, but their success has been hard won. When Wally's grandfather, Harry, and his family came out to Carbunup from England they were granted a farm and given 1000 pounds. What they were not told was that the 'farm' was virgin bush, and the 1000 pounds had to be paid back! However, Harry and his wife, Amelia, began the arduous task of carving a small family farm out of the dense forest. Wally's father, John, was 8 when they arrived in Australia, and his aunt, Kathleen, was 11. Wally's father and mother, Yvonne, continued to scrape a meagre living from the

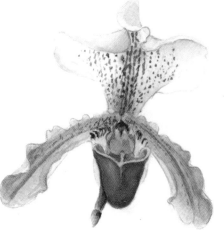

Now known as "the wine with the flowers" Anniebrook wines, made in a range of easy-drinking styles, have most attractive labels individually designed for each variety. Each bottle of wine is sold together with a little flower. The large selection of wines and the amazing array of artificial and silk flowers make this a fascinating destination that is unique in the area.

The name Anniebrook is taken from the small creek that meanders through the property, and in another little snippet of history the old Watermoor School, which used to be situated on the farm, was named after the road that Wally's father John and aunt Kathleen had walked along to school all those years ago in England.

land, but when Wally, one of seven children, inherited the farm, he also inherited the debt that went with it. He and Dawn were married in 1969 and managed to pay this off, but realised that to survive as farmers they would either have to buy a much larger property, or radically diversify their business. They were able to buy one farm next to their home block, but no others nearby wanted to sell. They looked at properties elsewhere around the State, but nowhere seemed as nice as where they lived!

So in 1986 they decided to intensify their operation, initially planting 5 acres to vines and 5 acres to flowers, mainly Proteas and Leucodendrons. This rapidly expanded and at one stage they had 20 acres of flowers! The dried flower trade was good at the time, and they used to dry, dye, sulphur and glycol all the surplus that couldn't be sold fresh. Dawn remembers starting on the kitchen table making mixed, fresh bunches, until a bench on the veranda was set up, thence to the double garage; finally a purpose-built shed was constructed! But the grapes gradually took over and 18 acres are now planted to vines. After years of selling their grapes to other wineries, in 2006 a dream was realised and they opened their cellar door with their own label of Anniebrook wines, complimenting the existing family-run flower emporium.

Wally and Dawn's third son, Andrew, is now the fourth generation of the Lewis family to live on the farm, making a living as a sheep farmer and, together with his wife, Serena, building and managing Cowaramup's childcare facility.

P.Negus

ARAVINA ESTATE

Established: 1996

This is a story in two parts. In its former life, Aravina was Amberley Estate, established by Bridget and Albert Haak with a group of family and friends, including the former owner of the land, dentist Michael Sturgeon. The Haaks had recently emigrated from South Africa and were wishing to establish a vineyard in the Margaret River area, having been told in glowing terms of its potential. After searching for several months Albert, a former agricultural engineer, thought that this piece of land, on a gently sloping block full of big Marri trees was just right, but it was not for sale. However, Michael had been looking for something to do with the block, and was persuaded to sell, but to come in as a shareholder.

Bridget's grandparents had named their farm in South Africa 'Amberley' after the village they had come from in Sussex, England. The new vineyard was in the Sussex location of the Busselton Shire, so to use this name for their winery seemed a very fitting connection. The impressive winery, cellar door, restaurant and gardens were built in a lovely setting, near the ridge top overlooking a sweeping valley and dam. Extensive gardens have always been one of the winery's attractions for visitors, especially the various varieties of hydrangeas planted around the little creek that flows down near the entrance. This is a haven for frogs, which are a sure indicator of a healthy environment. The tiny green frogs on the hydrangeas in the painting are baby 'motorbike' frogs, named for their throaty

call that sounds like a revving motorbike. A large number were found and photographed one day on a visit to the winery when they must have just emerged from their tadpole stage.

Amberley was sold to a large consortium, Constellation Wines, in 2004, but in 2010 was purchased by seventh generation West Australian, Steve Tobin, and his partner, Melissa Lynton-Lobato who coincidentally, were both born in the wheatbelt town of Katanning. The property has been renamed Aravina Estate by Melissa. After many years of running a successful seismic survey business, Steve is now finally able to start living his dream to create a unique facility that has a whole range of different attractions and activities where families can spend a whole day of relaxation and enjoyment. Their plans include an Equestrian Centre, a Sports Car Museum, tearooms over the lake, and an expanded gallery and function centre. Already the restaurant has had a 'makeover' and a state-of-the-art playground has been installed in the garden. Managers, Michael and Allison Kelly, who have been associated with the Margaret River Wine Industry for 30 years, oversaw much of this work. They are also long term friends as Steve and Mike went to school together in Perth.

One of Steve's delightful new additions is a beautifully crafted rowing boat, circa 1970, made from Tasmanian Huon Pine. You may need to look for it though, as it has been suspended from the ceiling in the cafe where the luscious

golden-brown colour of the aged wood contrasts well with the white ceiling.

For several years, the Amberley gardens provided a magnificent setting for a 'Semillon and Seafood' weekend, which used to be held regularly each February. In 2011 this popular festival has been resurrected, this time in April, when once again some of the best white wines and fine foods from around the region could be sampled and enjoyed by patrons.

P.Negus

BERRY FARM

Established: 1985

When Andrea and Eion Lindsay came to Margaret River in 1984, Andrea from Sydney and Eion from New Zealand, their plan was to buy a smallholding on which to establish a low-key market garden that would enable them to be self-sufficient. The old group settlement cottage that they found on Bessell Road, with its lovely gardens and over 100 acres of farmland, was an ideal location. The property was originally settled by pioneer Verna Vinall and her family during the 1920s. Verna named the property Thornhill after the family estate that she had left behind in England.

The trouble was, Andrea and Eion were too good at growing things! Their produce flourished on the rich soils, so they began to sell their excess at the local markets in Margaret River. People couldn't get enough; word got around and a trickle of friends and locals made trips out to the Lindsays' farm to buy whatever fruit and vegetables were in season: tomatoes, beans, capsicums, corn, and in time there were avocados, kiwi fruit, nuts and, of course, the various berries. As people milled around the cottage Andrea thought it would be a good idea to "flit around the garden" offering Devonshire teas with homemade jam. Little did she realize what she had started! The trickle soon became a flood, and the Berry Farm was born!

Initially, visitors were able to pick their own strawberries and to venture down to the creek for raspberries in season, but this was hard to manage and the potential for accidents was always a worry. With an eye for business, Andrea and Eion decided that the only viable way forward would be by 'value-adding', and so the range of jams, chutneys and pickles began to expand, making use of all their excess produce. Before long their first fruit wines were also produced. Eion remembers the 'flat' strawberry wine not looking too good, but when they purchased the region's first carbonator, the sparkling strawberry "champagne" became an instant hit. He built a small 'cave' into the hillside as a vinegary, and a range of fruit and herb vinegars was added to the Berry Farm list. As the business grew, production moved from the cramped conditions of the cottage kitchen to a new, purpose-built shed, and the family also moved to the less cramped rammed earth home they had built on the other side of the valley.

One might say that the Berry Farm business 'exploded' rather than expanded. But unfortunately growth required capital, and convincing the banks of the Berry Farm's potential was an almost impossible task. At the time, interest rates were horrendous, and as Andrea wryly quipped "We got the sack from every bank in town!" For some years the going was tough. Berry Farm produce, however, was finding its way into the Perth market, and the turn-around came when they were awarded a contract to supply the national retailer, David Jones. The Lindsays were finally able to obtain the finance they needed, and to continue with confidence and security, until "retirement" finally beckoned after 20 years in the business.

New Holland Honeyeaters feasting on strawberry jam

In 2006, the Berry Farm was purchased by the French family, who were looking to buy a hospitality business in the region for their daughter Rebecca. Being regular visitors to the farm they were thrilled to discover the Berry Farm on the market. Rebecca and partner, Michael Skivinis, took over the day-to-day management and were married in the cottage gardens the following year. Five years on and with two beautiful young daughters in tow, Michael and Rebecca have made many improvements to the infrastructure while keeping the original charm of the property.

Today the Berry Farm continues to thrive, with its huge range of delicious products, and peaceful ambience in the cottage café and garden. The Splendid Fairy-wrens, New Holland Honeyeaters and other small birds continue to delight visitors, as they have done since the Berry Farm's early days, when they first discovered the delicious taste of cream and strawberry jam!

Splendid Fairy-wrens just love cream

BETTENAY WINES

Established: 1989

There are definitely some trout in the lake at Bettenays, because Greg once caught a poacher with the proof! He does, however, stock the lake each year with several hundred plate-sized rainbow trout. Visitors staying in the cottages have 'fishing rights' and any fish caught are paid for on an honour system. There is nothing like a fresh trout for breakfast! Water birds also love the lake, and a family of Pacific Black Ducks is a common sight on the lake in spring. Other species include Wood Ducks, Mountain Ducks and Musk Ducks. A family of Black Swans visits for a few days every year.

However, the vineyard and winery don't leave Greg much time for fishing these days. In fact, at vintage it can become just a little too busy, sometimes necessitating working through the night to process the grapes. Greg once ended up in a hospital bed for a short while after one such 'Vintage Blitz', and was told by his doctor that he'd "lost the plot"! Well, of course, that just

became the theme, along with the Lost Plot Dog, for the second label of Bettenay Wines.

Some of Greg's colleagues in the wine industry might believe that he has, indeed, lost the plot, with such wines as the famous 'Chilli Rose' and 'Sweet Dreams', which are anything but traditional types of

P.Negus

Pacific Black Duck and young on Greg's lake

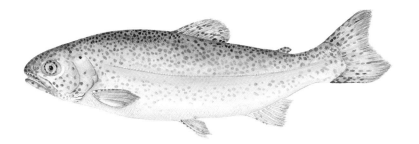

Rainbow trout

wine. However, Greg wanted to bring a touch of fun to his wines, and judging by the rate at which the bottles exit the cellar door, his customers think they are great fun too! Watch out for the jokes when Greg is playing host in the tasting area.

Greg has always been a 'workaholic'. When getting the vineyard established, he and his father dug in all the irrigation for the vines themselves – by hand. His dad, Eric, worked for the CSIRO mapping soils all over Western Australia, while Greg has an Honours Degree in Horticulture, so between them they had a fair idea of where to plant their grapes. To make ends meet, Greg also taught viticulture at TAFE in Margaret River and, running a tight schedule between vineyard and college, he was often known to be late for lectures! Practices in the vineyard did not always match the theory of the classroom, but nevertheless, Bettenay Premium Wines, are up there with the best, and have been consistent award winners, while the grapes, some of which are sold to bigger wineries, are always in high demand. Greg and his wife, Terri, still do much of the work themselves, but their son, Bryce, has now joined them and has adopted the mantle of winemaker. Bryce is also responsible for the delicious range of Bettenays Nougat that can be purchased at the cellar door.

Designed by architects, Des and Sophie Smith, the contemporary cellar door and tasting room has a beautiful view over the lake. A stylish spa apartment above makes a luxurious holiday getaway for couples, while two other cosy country cottages also have lake and vineyard views. Greg and Terri have plans to complete their complex with a small amphitheatre, restaurant and another small lake or two – one day.

Greg fishing for his and Terri's breakfast

BLACKWOOD MEADERY

Established: 1997

Mead is the oldest known fermented beverage, and its history can be traced back at least 9,000 years. It is made from honey, a food that would have been a popular delicacy from the earliest times, despite being rather tricky to obtain! Many animals, including bears of course, have been wise to this sweet treat for millions of years. One can easily understand how, with a little serendipity and lots of experimentation, early humans would have discovered the very agreeable drink that results from the natural fermentation of honey. Its production would then have been refined down the ages.

Archaeological evidence for mead production has been found in China, from pottery vessels containing mead, rice and fruits, dated to around 7000 BC. It was known by the Beaker People of Europe in the 3rd millennium BC, is recorded in the hymns of the Rig Veda from India, and in the writings of ancient Greece and the Roman Empire. Germanic tribes in

Plants particularly loved by bees

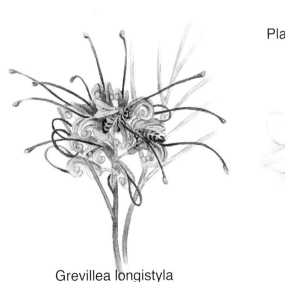

Grevillea longistyla

Choisya

Pincushion Hakea

Jarrah   Red-flowering Gum   Patterson's Curse

Northern Europe commonly brewed mead, in areas where it was too cold to grow grapes, and historical references to the honey brew are found all over Europe, as well as from Africa and Asia. A form of mead called tej is made today in Ethiopia, and in South Africa mead, known as iQhilika, is traditionally prepared by the Xhosa people. Mead has long been associated with revelry and romance, as it was a drink for special occasions. The word 'honeymoon' came from the tradition of drinking mead for a full cycle of the moon after the wedding.

There is a buzz of excitement at the meadery as Horst and Martha talk about their small operation, where they do almost everything themselves. They enjoy the challenge of introducing this drink of old civilizations to a new generation for whom it is relatively unknown. Drinking a drop of mead, Martha says, makes one think back on history, nature and life itself. In olden times, when everyday life was harsh, mead was seen as the giver of health, strength, wisdom, fertility and more, and it would have seemed like a godsend, so to speak, for survival. Honey is actually completely sterile and its healing properties are today once again being recognised.

Horst says he has the connoisseur in mind when producing his meads, and honeys are carefully selected to experience the delicate and different flavours of our native flora such as Jarrah, Marri, Karri and various wildflowers. The meads are made in dry, medium and sweet styles. Honey from Patterson's Curse has its own individual flavour, and is much sought after. When fermented it makes a dry and delicate mead wine. He also makes liqueur mead and a refreshing mead brew. Horst and Martha also combine honey with fruits, such as boysenberries, blueberries and plums, in combinations that were established in the early days of agriculture. Martha points out that finally, one must give credit to the magnificent bee without whose gift to mankind, we would find it hard to exist.

Horst and Martha with a selection of their mead and honey products

BROOKLAND VALLEY

Established: 1984

The little bronze statue that features on all the Brookland Valley wines is not Pan, but Daphnis, another flute-playing figure from Greek mythology. Pan, the half-man, half-goat god, does however, feature in his story.

Daphnis was the son of the Greek god Hermes, born to him by a nymph who he tricked into making love. She abandoned the baby in a grove of laurels (also known as Daphnes), but the goddess Hera saw this and made sure he was found by some shepherds who raised him as one of their own. Daphnis became renowned for both his beauty and his songs and poems. He was well loved by Pan, and it was he who taught Daphnis to play the panpipes. Daphnis fell in love with a beautiful nymph called Nomia, and she with him. However she had a rival, Chimaera, who one day plied Daphnis with wine and seduced him. At this, Nomia flew into a jealous rage and caused Daphnis to go blind. The legend tells how, for the remainder of his life, the heartbroken Daphnis took to flute playing with new passion, his music now sadder and more beautiful than ever before.

The bronze Daphnis that sits in the garden at Brookland Valley originally resided in the garden of a stately home that was purchased by the National Trust. They were unable to maintain all the gardens, and the statue was sold at auction in Sydney. Daphnis was purchased by Brookland Valley Vineyard, which now makes a perfect home for the little flute-player pictured here accompanied by a Golden Whistler.

Hopefully, those who drink Brookland Valley wines will not suffer the same fate as Daphnis. However, visitors should take care, as the beautiful cellar door, wine arts gallery and restaurant, overlooking a picturesque lake in the Wilyabrup valley, certainly lends itself to encounters of love and seduction.

Daphnis and a male Golden Whistler making music together

BROOKWOOD ESTATE

Established: 1996

Owners, Lyn and Trevor Mann, have always done everything on a tight budget at Brookwood Estate, using second-hand and fixed-up equipment, and lots of tenacity. It all began when Trevor, who had grown up on a farm, wanted to go back to agriculture after working for years in car yards with a panel beating business in Perth. Lyn, a hairdresser, was happy to go to the country but did not want to go to the wheatbelt. It so happened that just as they were thinking this way, the Manns won a holiday, through Trevor's work, and decided to take it down south. Like many before them, they fell in love with the Margaret River region and decided that was where they would like to be. They bought their block in 1996 and their first plantings were in September of that year.

The Manns began to establish their vineyard, using pruned vine cuttings gathered from the best vineyards in the region, and an old Fordson tractor that is still the vineyard workhorse today. The Manns had poured all their savings into their property. Trevor worked at Busselton Toyota for the first few years to make ends meet, while Lyn learned winemaking in 'hands-on' fashion, working with Neil Gallagher at Woody Nook. Neil made their wines for the first few years until Lyn felt more confident. They then bought the Gallaghers' old horizontal basket press (illustrated in action), a magnificent piece of equipment that had originally come from the Loire Valley in France. Basket presses may be horizontal or upright, and are ideal for dealing with small quantities of fruit. They extract the grape juice much more gently than large pneumatic air-bag presses that are more suited to processing large volumes. The crusher, that had previously seen service at Plantagenet Wines, was also acquired from Woody Nook. Lyn was now ready to make her own wines.

Lyn and Trevor's daughter, Bronnley, after graduating from Margaret River High School, studied winemaking at Curtin University in Perth, thus bringing a little more theoretical 'know-how' into the family business. All Brookwood wines are still made today from their own fruit in their winery by mum and daughter team, Lyn and Bronnley Mann. This is an unusual achievement for a small winery that often involves family and close friends crushing the grapes in the middle of the night, so that they can operate the cellar door and café next day!

The café has always been a feature of Brookwood, specialising in heavily laden gourmet platters, homemade dukkah, and home-cooked soups. These are served on the enclosed veranda overlooking the vines, where an old slow-combustion stove keeps customers warm in winter.

Matt and Trevor sampling must crushed from cabernet sauvignon,
using one of Australia's oldest working horizontal basket presses, dating from 1960

BROWN HILL ESTATE

Established: 1994

It's a far cry from the West Australian Goldfields to a vineyard at Margaret River. When Jim Bailey bought his block of land at Rosa Brook, he called it Brown Hill because it reminded him of the place of that name where he grew up, on the 'Golden Mile' 5 km south east of Kalgoorlie. Gold was discovered there in 1893 by Fred Cammilleri, and it turned out to be one of the goldfield's richest finds. Hannans Brown Hill Gold Mining Company was one of the first floated in Kalgoorlie in 1894, and the town was gazetted in 1899. It became a bustling mining town with a strong community complete with schools and churches.

Four generations of the Bailey family lived in the Goldfields with strong ties to Brown Hill. Growing up on the Goldfields, Jim used to water the vegetable patch with his father by diverting water from the old mine workings there. The town of Brown Hill no longer exists today, as it has been swallowed up by the Kalgoorlie Super Pit, but many of the names of places

from around the area, as well as some of the miners, have been immortalized in the names of the Brown Hill wines. The name 'Fimiston', their Reserve Shiraz, was taken from another old settlement that has since vanished into the Super Pit, and the Pit actually takes its name from that town. 'Chaffers' Shiraz was named after the deepest mine in the vicinity, and 'Croesus' Merlot came from the plant where the gold was treated. Jim, and his son Nathan, have a book and map showing the names of all the old mines on the Golden Mile.

Jim Bailey and his wife, Gwen, who also comes from a fourth generation family from Kalgoorlie, where she was a geological draftswoman, had a shoe shop in Mundaring for many years, before fulfilling a long-held dream to make wine on their Rosa Brook block. Jim bought an ancient tractor for a slab of beer. That tractor still works, though he does use a newer model now. The painting shows the old tractor, together with some Common Bronzewings that have flown in from the nearby bushland. The tractor was the last one made by the David Brown Company, which then changed direction somewhat, going on to acquire the Aston Martin and Lagonda car companies!

The vineyard and winery is owned jointly with Nathan, who along with managing the business is also the winemaker, while his wife, Chiara, looks after the accounts. All the family is involved in running their very successful enterprise. Brown Hill has gained a great reputation for a small winery, and was named Small Producer of the year in Ray Jordan's WA Wine Guide for two years in a row in 2009 and 2010.

The Brown Hill wine label design shows the stylised shape of the hill behind the winery that reminded Jim so much of his old home, with the cross hatching representing the rows of grape vines. There is no special cellar door at Brown Hill. Visitors to the winery are greeted at the friendly 'no-frills' wooden tasting counter inside the winery shed where all the work takes place. The Baileys' motto is to 'Keep it Simple', concentrating just on producing the highest quality wines at reasonable prices.

Their John Brown tractor and disk-plough with Bronzewing Pigeons in the foreground

CAPE GRACE WINES

Established: 1996

When Robert & Karen Karri-Davies saw a Great Egret on their vineyard dam it was quite a surprise. These handsome birds are more usually found further north, on the wide, flat seasonal wetlands of the Vasse Estuary. They were so impressed with their sighting that they chose the egret as an emblem for their wine labels.

On a visit to Cape Grace you are more likely to see the small bush birds, such as Splendid Fairy-wrens, Scarlet Robins and New Holland Honeyeaters that inhabit the lovely area of Jarrah forest surrounding the winery and cellar door building. Bands of Black Cockatoos, both Red- and White-tailed, visit occasionally, and may obligingly drop a feather or two.

It is fitting that Cape Grace should nestle

amongst the trees. Robert's great grandfather was Maurice Coleman Davies, founder of the prosperous timber empire that flourished in the Capes region from the 1880s to the early 1900s. MC Davies also built the impressive lighthouse, opened in 1896 that stands at the tip of Cape Leeuwin. Timber was the major industry here then, and thousands of tons of Jarrah and Karri logs were exported from Hamelin Bay and Augusta to destinations all over the world. Many of London's streets were paved with timber from the South West. There were mills operating at various times at Kudardup, Jarrahdene, and Boranup, with the largest and most permanent at Karridale. At its height, the industry supported up to 1000 people and even printed its own currency. MC Davies' family

Great Egret

home at Karridale was later moved, lock stock and barrel, to Margaret River, where it now houses the restaurant in the Grange-on-Farrelly Motel.

Most of the trees in the magnificent Karri forest of Boranup, a short drive south of Cape Grace, are now a little over 100 years old, having re-grown since that time of feverish activity in the late 19th century. Today at Cape Grace, Robert and Karen are keen to preserve the forested section of their property that provides a sheltered and picturesque setting for one of Margaret River's smallest vineyards. They use minimal sprays and no insecticides, opting instead for a small flock of guinea fowl to keep the insects at bay. Cape Grace employs traditional winemaking techniques, with the reds being hand plunged and basket pressed. Their wines are sold primarily at the cellar door and by mail order. Robert is a self-taught vigneron, a change of direction for him after leaving a profession in commercial and industrial photography spanning 20 years. Karen's extensive background in marketing has been a very useful and necessary skill, as they try to keep ahead in an increasingly competitive industry.

If history had been different, Cape Grace might have grown grapes much earlier. This plot of land was Dr. Tom Cullity's first choice when he was searching for a location in which to trial vines in the 1960s. However, at that time it was not for sale, and he settled instead for a block a few kilometres further north, where he established the Margaret River Wine Region's first commercial vineyard at Vasse Felix.

CAPE MENTELLE

Established: 1970

Cape Mentelle, established by David and Sandy Hohnen, was one of the pioneer vineyards of the Margaret River Wine Region. It followed closely on the heels of Vasse Felix and Cullen Wines. Cape Mentelle put Margaret River on the international wine map when it became the first West Australian producer to win the prestigious Jimmy Watson Trophy at the 1983 Melbourne Wine Show for its 1982 Cabernet Sauvignon. It won again the following year.

David's brother Giles, an artist and house designer, and architect, Tom Roberts, saw great potential in the use of local sand, gravel and clay soils as an environmentally friendly building material. They thought that Cape Mentelle's winery building would make an ideal prototype. Earth walls have traditionally been used in many parts of the world, but were long ago replaced in the west by kiln-fired bricks and other materials. By adding a little cement to the mix, Giles and Tom were convinced that rammed earth walls would be durable enough to withstand the wet, south west winters. They should be relatively cheap to build, strong and low maintenance, and the thick walls would ensure internal temperature stability, an important consideration for a winery. This original shed still forms the core of the much-expanded winery today. The winery building and the Cape Mentelle homestead were the first rammed earth buildings in the State to be given planning permission. Others quickly followed, and today both rammed earth and mud brick are popular choices of building material all over Australia.

Today Cape Mentelle, as part of Estates & Wines (owned by Moët Hennessy Louis Vuitton) continues to build on its solid foundations. The winery is only 3 km from the town of

Margaret River, and offers tours of both winery and vineyard in conjunction with gourmet lunch platters. It hosts a very popular annual Cabernet tasting, and currently holds a festival of outdoor movies through the warm summer months.

Geese have always been part of the scene at Cape Mentelle and are often to be seen nibbling the grass around the cellar door or between the rows of vines. These geese have developed discerning palates, however, with a particular liking for premium Cabernet grapes. This habit does lessen their popularity with the vineyard manager and winemaker, but they are forgiven for the sake of their charm!

The winery takes its name from the nearby limestone headland that lies between the mouth of the Margaret River and Kilcarnup to the north. Like many natural features along the south west coast, this was named by Nicholas Baudin, leader of the 1801 French expedition of exploration to Australia. It commemorates two notable French scientists, geographer Edmund and his cartographer brother, Francois-Simon Mentelle, who lived in Paris in the early 1700s. The Cape actually consists of three cliffy points, two of which enclose a beautiful semi-circular bay. Its shape has inspired the local name of Wineglass Bay, but maybe there is a double connection here!

The Geese at Cape Mentelle enjoying premium Cabernet grapes

CAPE NATURALISTE VINEYARD

Established: 1997

The beautifully renovated old buildings at Cape Naturaliste Vineyard have a very long history. The homestead, now home to vineyard owners, Craig and Jennifer Brent-White, was originally a coach inn in the 1860s for travellers journeying between Perth and the Bussell family home of Wallcliffe House. In those days there was very little white settlement between the town of Vasse (now Busselton) and Augusta, which was established in 1831. Pastoralists such as the Bussells gradually took up land along the coast, but the Capes area was sparsely populated and the "roads" were rough dirt tracks, sandy in summer and muddy in winter.

In 1883 the property, which at the time extended from Injidup Road up to Yallingup along both sides of Caves Road, became a dairy farm, and the homestead was relocated to its present position from further down the valley, where it had been subject to flooding. It was then called Thorn Hill. The Gunyulgup Valley was excellent for farming, having rich alluvial soils, permanent underground springs, and shelter from the prevailing winds. This was the era of commercial whaling and American ships regularly plied the south west coast in search of Humpback and Southern Right Whales (so named because they were the 'right' ones to catch, being slow-swimming, floated when dead, and yielded large amounts of valuable oil). The whaleboats would anchor in the relative shelter of Smiths Beach to purchase vegetables from the farm.

Laurance has its Chick on a Stick,
Cowramup has its Rump on a Stump,
Cape Naturaliste has its Dog on A Log (Monty).

As with old buildings everywhere, the Cape Naturaliste property has its legends, and the following is supported by documentation. An aboriginal farm worker named 'Winjee Sam' was rather well known as a 'Ladies' man' and may have been enjoying a relationship with the farmer's wife. In a fit of jealousy, the farmer took his gun down to the coast in search of Sam, whom he found fishing at Torpedo Rocks, and shot him dead. Such incidents were often turned a blind-eye to by neighbours in those days, but this gentleman was unlucky to be charged and finally brought to trial in 1899. However, the records show that he was found "Not guilty", his defence being that he had mistaken the victim for a seal!

The property remained an active dairy farm, under various ownerships, for nearly 100 years, until a mining company purchased the land in 1970 after the valley had been discovered to be rich in mineral sands. Luckily, however, the government denied mining rights and vested a large part of the property as an 'A' Class Reserve, which was later incorporated into the Leeuwin-Naturaliste National Park.

When you find this hidden little vineyard gem, you are probably visiting Australia's most western vineyard. Jennifer and Craig Brent-White manage Cape Naturaliste Vineyard using a biodynamic approach, spreading compost, planting cover crops, and spraying kelp and trace elements. In 2008, they won a Geo Catch award for environmental improvements to the property, they planted over 23,000 trees shrubs and native flowers in 2005, and several of its wines have been gold medal winners. The old dairy building has been restored and now functions as the tasting room. How much more appealing today to see here a successful vineyard and farm, surrounded by natural bushland, than the aftermath of an open-cut strip mine.

In the early days most farms had one or two Jersey cows; house-cows for cream and milk

CHURCHVIEW ESTATE

Established: 1999

Owner of Churchview Estate, Spike Fokkema, tells how he and two mates used to cycle down on rather old and heavy bikes from Perth to Margaret River for their holidays when they were teenagers. This was soon after Spike's family had emigrated to Western Australia from Holland in 1954. The trip took 5 days and their total budget was 15 shillings ($1.50) a day. That was so little that lunch did not happen.

Their faces fell when they arrived at the new Prevelly Campground and were told the camping fee was 5 shillings (50 cents) per night. This would have somewhat strained their resources. Camping rough in the bush was contemplated; however a reprieve was won with the promise of a free site in exchange for the boys distributing brochures around Perth when they returned home. As a result of this promotion, many of their extended family and friends have spent repeated holidays at Prevelly Park since those early days!

In much earlier days still, the old farm at Churchview was home to Group Settlers when the land was first opened up to white settlement in the early 1920s. The aim of the Group Settlement Scheme, the brainchild of Sir James Mitchell, was to establish a dairy industry in the South West to supply the growing population of Perth. Groups of new migrants from the United Kingdom, after a crash course in dairy farming back home, were allocated land from which to clear the forest, build homes and graze their cattle. Most of the migrants were from city backgrounds and were unprepared for the backbreaking work of clearing the dense Jarrah and Karri forest. The Great Depression descended soon after the start of the scheme, adding to the hardships faced by the settlers, and many eventually walked off their land. However, much of today's cleared farmland is the result of their labours, and some of the old 'Groupie' cottages remain. The cellar door at Churchview Estate is not the original cottage, but was built in 1954. In 1998 the cottage was restored and finished in the same traditional Group

Settlement cottage style. There is certainly a historic feeling as you walk into the restored building to taste Churchview's wines, or maybe just to sip a glass of Chardonnay on the timber veranda as you watch the world go by.

Churchview Estate takes its name from the heritage-listed St. John the Baptist Anglican Church, located just opposite the winery, on the west side of the Bussell Highway. This little church would have been the focus of the community in the early days, and it would have seen quite a few Group Settlement weddings, such as the one pictured here. Regular services are still held there, and the church is still a popular venue for wedding ceremonies today.

A Group-Settlement wedding at Metricup Church

CLAIRAULT WINES

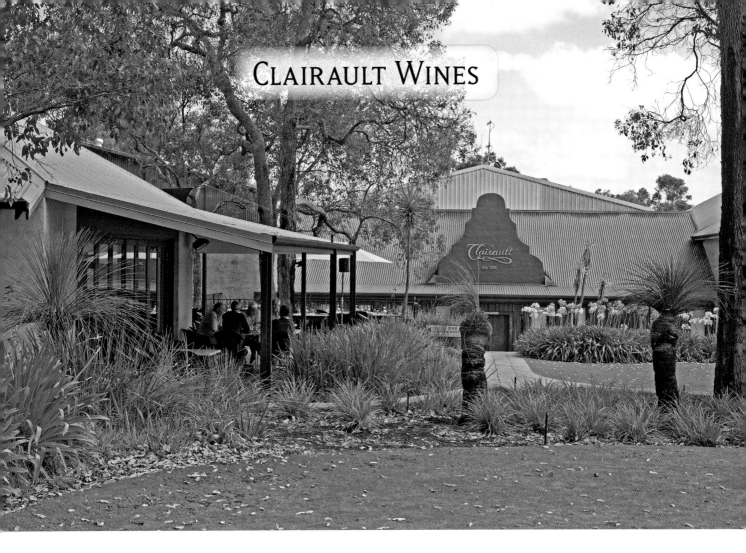

Established: 1976

What does a French mathematician have to do with a Margaret River winery?

In the late 18th and early 19th century, several French voyages were made to explore and survey the coastline of the mysterious "Great South Land" as Australia was then known. From 1801 to 1803, Captain Nicholas Baudin commanded a scientific expedition to chart its coast with two ships, the *Geographe* and the *Naturaliste*. At that time it was not even clear whether Australia was one large landmass or if there was an inland sea dividing the continent in two. At the same time, during this period of frenzied exploration, a British expedition, led by Matthew Flinders, was also charting the coast of Australia, and it was he who first successfully circumnavigated the continent. The two nations jostled for supremacy through their respective expeditions, but eventually it was Great Britain that laid claim to the whole of Australia. However, the French named many prominent features around the south west coast of Western Australia, including Cape Clairault, which lies 10 km south of Yallingup.

Baudin named this cape after Alexis Claude Clairaut (1713 – 1765). He was a renowned French mathematician who, among other things, had helped to calculate the length of the meridian of Paris. He had also calculated the perihelion of Halley's comet, successfully predicting its return in 1759. The difference in spelling – the Cape is "Clairault" - was an error made later by the French cartographers. The Cape's location didn't fare too well either, as the original spot chosen for the name was a few kilometres further north between Canal Rocks and Smiths Beach. Here high granite cliffs are clearly visible, whereas Cape Clairault itself is too low to be distinguished from out at sea. However, with its steep, north-facing sand dune, it is the most prominent feature that you see when looking south from anywhere further north along the coast.

Clairault Winery and Vineyard was one of the earliest to be established in the Wilyabrup sub-region, soon after Vasse Felix, Cullens and Moss Wood. Ian Lewis was a geologist who, after working in the north of the state, was looking for a cooler way of making a living. His wife, Ani, from South Africa, inspired the Cape Dutch style of the original cellar door and winery building. From the outset, the Lewis' wanted to work with nature on their vineyard, and maintained corridors of bush to provide shelter for the predators of vineyard pests. Hawks that discouraged the grape-eating silvereyes nested in the tall trees nearby, and lizards living amongst the leaf litter kept the caterpillars at bay.

Now owned by the Martin family, Clairault has expanded more recently, but an environmentally responsible approach to vineyard management is their priority also, and beautiful bushland still surrounds the vines. The new cellar door and restaurant dovetail beautifully into the original building, which is now used for administration.

$$d = a\cos^{-1}[c \ldots \cos(\lambda_1 - \lambda_2) + \sin\delta_1\sin\delta_2]$$

$$\Delta\hat{\sigma} = \text{arcco} \ldots \phi_f + \cos\phi_s\cos\phi_f\cos\Delta\lambda)$$

$$\Delta\hat{\sigma} = 2\text{arcsi} \ldots \frac{\phi}{2}) + \cos\phi_s\cos\phi_f\sin^2\left(\frac{\Delta\lambda}{2}\right))$$

P.Negus

Alexis Claude Clairaut with calculations of latitude and longitude

CULLEN WINES

Established: 1967

When Dr. Kevin and Diana Cullen planted a trial plot of vines on their beef and sheep farm at Wilyabrup in 1966, a year before the first commercial planting at Vasse Felix next door, these first pioneers of Margaret River's wine industry had no inkling of where it would lead. Their planting was on the advice of Dr. John Gladstones, from the WA Department of Agriculture. He recognised that the Capes region bore many similarities to the Bordeaux wine region in France, having soils and climate that made it, potentially, an ideal area for producing top quality wines.

Forty years on, with well over 100 wineries and vineyards in the region, Cullen Wines is still one of the area's leading producers*. They continue to be a close-knit family operation, leading the way not only in the wine industry in general, but specifically in the philosophy of biodynamic farming. Right from the beginning, Kevin and Diana had strong environmental ideals, aiming to work in sympathy with the land, and to use minimal intervention with chemicals. Daughter, and winemaker since 1989, Vanya, has taken this philosophy to the highest level, with Cullen Wines achieving biodynamic certification in 2005. The quality of the grapes is seen as the key factor, and the wines are made by handling the fruit as little and as gently as possible. Biodynamic techniques take vineyard management beyond organic principles alone, embracing the whole of life, which includes not only the vines, the soils and the physical aspects of the vineyard, but also the rhythms of sun,

"How you spread goodwill is through giving good wine to people & they can socialize, relax their tensions & be happy"

Diana Madeline Cullen

2002

Boobook owl at Cullens

moon and planets, and the people who work there. This is what Vanya sees as the true meaning of 'Terroir'. Vineyard operations such as planting and harvesting are planned wherever possible to coincide with favourable positions of the moon, thought to be especially propitious when it is opposite Saturn.

As well as large quantities of compost, special preparations are used to enhance the growth of the vines, and these are applied at particular times through the year. Preparation 500, a manure fertilizer that has been buried over winter in cow horns, is sprayed onto the ground when the moon is descending, and during the afternoon when the earth is breathing in. It is sometimes mixed with fish emulsion and seaweed. Preparation 501 is a light enhancer consisting of ground quartz crystals that, after being similarly buried for several months, is sprayed onto the foliage of the vines, preferably on an ascending moon.

Cullen Wines is certainly a healthy vineyard, full of beneficial insects and birds. Members of staff were delighted when a Boobook Owl took up residence for a few months amongst the restaurant veranda rafters. Although the diet of owls consists chiefly of small birds and mammals, the Boobook, more than any other owl species, loves to eat insects. Evidently the Cullen vineyard won this owl's tick of approval.

* At the time of writing, Cullen Wines 2007 Kevin John Chardonnay has been judged best in the world by the Decanter World Wine Awards 2010.

Picking grapes on the full-moon

EDWARDS WINES

Established: 1994

One of the unique aspects of many of our Margaret River wineries is the amazing stories that belong to their owners. And none could be more extraordinary than that of the late Brian Edwards and his 1943 Tiger Moth, Matilda.

Brian had long held a dream to fly a Tiger Moth solo from England to Australia, following in the footsteps of aviation pioneers, Bert Hinkler and Sir Charles Kingsford Smith. His father, a Lancaster bomber pilot, had been killed in action in World War II, and he and his family had been cared for by Legacy, the charity that looks after dependants of deceased servicemen. Brian wanted to repay this debt, and to honour his father's memory, as well as to experience the trials and the thrills of flying the Kangaroo Route to Australia solo, in a biplane, as the early aviators had done.

The story of the 'Matilda Mission', in which Brian Edwards describes his solo flight across the world in 1990, is a gripping read. Battling with bureaucracies, dealing in turn with numbing cold and searing heat, rain squalls, hail and dust storms, being blown off course by gale-force winds, and forced down into unknown territory by mechanical problems were just some of the difficulties that he encountered. Navigation was by compass and map held tightly in one hand - to prevent it blowing away - while searching for recognizable features, such as a river valley or mountain range, coastal inlet or cape. These were often few and far between, and sometimes the map was just a white blank stamped "Data Incomplete".

There were a host of memorable highlights during this amazing flight, and Brian particularly remembered twice flying in the company of eagles that shadowed his plane, firstly over Saudi Arabia and then again over the Gulf of Kutch. There is an interesting connection here, as back in Perth Brian had been inaugural physiotherapist to the West Coast Eagles football team, (a role he held when they won the AFL Premiership in

Wedge-tailed Eagle

1992 and 1994). And before each home game at Subiaco, a trained Wedge-tailed Eagle flies around the oval over the crowd.

A major change in lifestyle occurred in 1992 when Brian and Jenny bought land near Margaret River on which to develop a vineyard. Their first vines were planted in 1994, and the small cellar door opened for business in 2000. Brian's flight from London to Perth is featured on the wine labels, and the decommissioned Tiger Moth now sits for visitors to admire in a hanger just behind the cellar door building.

Sadly, Brian passed away in 2003 from leukaemia, but the winery continues to be run today by his sons, Michael as winemaker and Christo as viticulturist. Brian had been made a life member of The West Coast Eagles in 2003, a privilege that has been extended to Jenny since his death. Sitting on the veranda one day, Brian was watching a hawk. He turned to Jenny and told her: " In my next life if I have to come back as something I would love to come back as a hawk." Quickly realizing what he had said, he added "the feathered variety of course!"

The Tiger Moth flown by Brian Edwards
that is on show at the winery

FIRETAIL WINES

Established: 2002

Jessica Worrall and Rob Glass did not come to Margaret River for the quiet life. Both had busy jobs as engineers, but were keen to amalgamate their professional backgrounds with their passion for wine. They bought a small vineyard near

Capel in 1999, planting Merlot vines and producing their first vintage in 2003. In 2002 they purchased their dream property at Rosa Glen near Margaret River. This was originally planted by the Lindsay family, who had also established and developed The Berry Farm next door. Their vines are mature, having been planted in 1980, and the rammed earth homestead enjoyed views over the vineyard.

Rosa Glen is a lovely rural part of the Margaret River region, with rolling hills and farms interspersed with natural bushland. It has a rich history too, being first opened up in the group settlement days after the First World War. When you visit Firetail Wines, take time to have a look at the old CWA Hall and Pioneer Settlers' Memorial on the corner of Rosa Glen and Lucas Roads, only a few minutes drive from the cellar door.

As well as bringing the vineyard up to scratch, winemaking, building a cellar door outlet and marketing their new label, Jessica and Rob were juggling jobs. Rob still works much of the time overseas and Jessica is undertaking a Master's degree in Viticulture and Wine Technology externally through the University of Melbourne. They do have help with the vineyard and winemaking, so that they can focus attention on the marketing side of their business. The welcoming cellar door building of Jarrah and French Oak from old barrels has a delightfully warm feel. Local artworks line the walls, and a coffee machine hides behind the counter. Visitors are invited to sample the medal winning wines or enjoy a cup of coffee on the peaceful veranda overlooking the vines, or in winter on the comfortable couch inside. Young daughter, Amelia, presides over the retail wood products, attractive serving boards, candle and bottle holders made from oak barrel staves, and twig hooks from vine prunings.

When they can, Jessica and Rob get out into the vineyard, and Jessica is currently engaged in an experiment into the effects of various leaf-plucking strategies, a project for her Master's degree. They are gradually planting out beds of reeds and sedges to filter sediment and nutrients from the vineyard rainwater runoff before the water enters the dam, and a team of guinea fowl are now employed to keep the various weevil, snail and black beetle pests under control. These also act as rather vocal night watchmen, and do tend to drown out the soft 'wheee' of the Red-eared Firetail finches that are a feature of the property, and which inspired the name. Just occasionally, Jessica and Rob take a breath to enjoy the quiet life of Rosa Glen, and sit down with a glass of wine to listen to the birds and smell the roses.

Firetail Finches with Kings Park Bottlebrush

FLYING FISH COVE

Established: 1997

In the beginning, 22 small vineyard owners pooled their resources to share a winery facility in which to produce their wine. This quickly grew into a fully-fledged, specialist contract winemaking business, making wines not only for the original shareholders, but also for many other small vineyards in the Margaret River Wine Region. Located as they were, in the heart of Margaret River's Wilyabrup sub-region, it was not long before they decided to establish their own wine brand, Flying Fish Cove. In fact, the main fruit source for Flying Fish wines comes from the vineyard of the neighbouring Wildberry Farm, that some of the shareholders planted right at the outset

in 1997. The winery was constructed in 2000. They produced their first vintage in 2001, and in 2003 the first wines under the Flying Fish Cove name were released. These have since won several awards, and in 2005 and 2007 the winery was awarded most successful exhibitor under 300 tonnes in the Perth Royal Show.

Flying Fish, however, is not just about the wine. Understandably, most of the shareholders are all keen surfers, the winery being located so close to the wonderful South West Capes Coast. The Margaret River Wine Region is unique in being surrounded on three sides by the Indian and Southern

Damon Eastaugh, surfing a 55ft wave at Cow Bombie

Oceans, and some of the area's most spectacular surf breaks are only a stone's throw away. Chief winemaker, Damon Eastaugh, was one of the first to discover a 'secret' deep-water reef break, about 2 km offshore, that they called Cow Bombie. The waves here can reach Hawaiian proportions, and it is now famous throughout the surfing community! In 2006 Damon won the ASL (Australian Surfing Life) Oakley Big Wave Award for riding a huge wave here, estimated at approximately 50 feet.

Conditions along the Capes Coast are very special for surf. Of course, the whole of the West Coast of Australia faces the huge expanse of the Indian Ocean where there is time for waves to build up uninterrupted for thousands of kilometres. But the Capes Coast itself juts far out into the ocean meeting the waves head-on. It is formed from a basement block of very ancient (2000 to 650 million year old) granitic and metamorphic rocks that are highly resistant, remaining in place while the softer rocks of the land further north have been eroded away. Together with the overlying, much younger limestone, mostly less than 1 million years old, these granitic rocks form the Leeuwin-Naturaliste Ridge. Much of the Ridge is now protected in the Leeuwin-Naturaliste National Park, ensuring that the beautiful natural scenery of the coastline is preserved for all to enjoy, and providing a complimentary backdrop to the attractive rural landscape of the vineyards and farms to the east.

GRALYN ESTATE

Established: 1975

In 1968 Merilyn and Graham Hutton married and moved to Wilyabrup. Graham had come from a dairy farming background and Merilyn was a home economics teacher at Busselton Senior High School. They had met at Junior Farmers, a club for rural youth.

They spent their first few years of marriage clearing their 230 hectare bush block, fencing, planting pasture and raising beef cattle, but the early 1970s were particularly tough with beef prices very low, so they made a decision to diversify into viticulture, and in 1975 planted a small area of the farm, 4.5 hectares, to grape vines. This decision came about partly after they were won over by a bottle of local 1973 Cabernet Sauvignon. Even in those early days, the Huttons realised that there was something very special about Wilyabrup grapes, and thought they would like to make wine.

The Huttons were self-taught winemakers, with Merilyn's knowledge of chemistry plus a few short wine quality control courses at the University of WA and lots of reading, providing the foundation for their new career. Graham's great sense of practicality made possible the vineyard planting and the building of a winery on the cheap, initially using wax lined concrete tanks and dairy coolers, a lot of self-help and improvisation. Merilyn recalls mixing the 9 tonnes of concrete in a small cement mixer for the walls of the winery. Graham split the 1800 vineyard posts and strainers from Jarrah trees on the property. In 1978, the year of their first vintage, they opened the region's first cellar door sales outlet, and christened their label 'Gralyn', a combination of their Christian names.

In 1978 the Huttons also made 136 litres of Vintage Port. Each of the three Hutton children were given a tonne of grapes to make a Port to mark the year of their 21st birthdays. This unusual gift involved them in all aspects of wine making – from picking grapes to designing their own wine labels. Today Gralyn Estate is well known for their range of high quality fortified wines, as well as a large selection of sweet wines and premium dry red wines.

They have won many awards for their wines. Perhaps one of the most memorable was won for the 1999 Shiraz Cabernet. This wine was judged Best Western Australian Table Wine at the 2000 SGIO Winemakers' Awards. The prize was two return air tickets from Perth to Rome or Paris, plus $1000 spending money. This gave Merilyn and Graham the chance to visit Bordeaux and increase their wine knowledge.

An interesting acquisition for the winery was a gypsy wagon that was previously owned by Vardo Horse-Drawn Holidays that operated out of Forest Grove just south of Margaret River in the 1980s. This landmark graced the entrance to Gralyn Estate from 1990 to 2002, and now features on the label of one of their special fortified dessert wines, Pedro Ximenez.

Merilyn and Graham have always believed the customer's wine-tasting experience is central to Gralyn Estate, and in 2002 a new tasting room was opened; a state-of-the-art facility,

Merilyn and Graham enjoying a drop of Gralyn red. Annette's dog Charlie is keeping watch

with superb views over the vines and surrounding farmland. The contemporary design is attributed to eldest son Michael, an architect; son Bradley is Gralyn winemaker, and daughter, Annette, is cellar door manager. Merilyn and Graham gain great satisfaction and pride from their achievements, and consider themselves fortunate in having their family involved in the business, and to have had loyal staff over Gralyn's 36 years of operation.

HAMELIN BAY WINES

Picture courtesy of Hamelin Bay Wines

Established: 1992

Hamelin Bay is a new winery, but proprietors, Ros and Richard Drake-Brockman, both have old family histories. The lineages of the Drakes and the Brockmans can be traced in Britain back to medieval times. They came together in 1761 by way of marriage, when Caroline Brockman married the Rev. Ralph Drake. At the time there were no sons in the Brockman family, and the name was in danger of dying out. In an astute move, Caroline's father would only give consent to the marriage if the Drake and Brockman names were joined.

Both Ros (nee Viveash) and Richard are fifth generation West Australians, whose families came out to the Swan River Colony soon after the settlement was established. The Drake-Bockmans arrived in 1830 and were allocated land in the Swan Valley, while the Viveashs settled in the Toodyay area in 1838. Richard's great grandfather, Frederick, was a surveyor and explorer, who travelled widely in the Pilbara and the Kimberleys. In 1882 he married Grace Bussell, one of the daughters of Alfred and Ellen, who built Ellensbrook Homestead and later, Wallcliffe House. Alfred was the youngest of four brothers who were amongst the first white settlers to arrive at Augusta in 1830. They later moved to Vasse, now Busselton, where the grazing land was better, but Alfred, with his new wife, Ellen, decided to start afresh at Ellensbrook in 1857. Grace is renowned for her part in the rescue

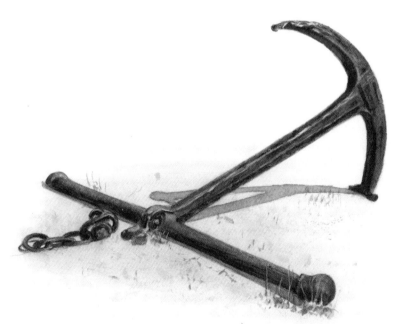

The Lovespring's anchor at Hamelin Bay

A Wyvern, a winged dragon

Fittingly, Hamelin Bay Wines lies snugly between the Bussell and Brockman Highways (access is off Brockman Highway), with the cellar door overlooking a steep, picturesque valley. It is only a few kilometres from Hamelin Bay, which is itself steeped in history, this time from the era of the 1890s when the timber industry dominated the economy of the area. Karridale was then a settlement of around 1000 people, and Hamelin Bay was a bustling port with a jetty that was eventually extended to 1800ft, exporting timber around the world. Unfortunately it was very open to North West winds, and the Bay became the site of many shipwrecks, including three, "Lovespring", "Katinka" and "Norwester", on one night alone in July 1900. The port was abandoned a few years later. The painting shows a Pied Cormorant on the remains of the jetty.

The anchor that is displayed near the boat ramp is from the "Lovespring".

of 60 survivors from the shipwrecked 'Georgette' on Calgardup (Redgate) Beach in 1876. After reading about her great courage in this rescue, Frederick was so impressed that he rode 300 km on horseback in order to meet her!

Hamelin Bay's wine labels feature a 'Wyvern', a mythological reptilian beast with a dragon's head and wings, the hindquarters of a snake or lizard, and a barbed tail. This legendary creature is the centrepiece of the Drake family crest. Both the Drakes and the Wyvern had strong connections with the west of England and South Wales, its name being drawn from two rivers, the Wye and the Severn, which both have their sources in the Welsh mountains and flow into the Bristol Channel.

A Pied Cormorant on
the remains of Hamelin Jetty

P.Negus

HAPPS

Established: 1978

Today, the winery, pottery and vineyard complex at Happs, on the slopes looking down towards Geographe Bay, is a far cry from the bare, wind-swept hillside above Dunsborough that teachers, Ros and Erl Happ, bought in 1975. The soft lines of the extruded mud brick buildings, and colourful entry and courtyard gardens welcome visitors to this popular venue. The two businesses of ceramics and wine go hand in hand, and are very much a family affair, with Jacquie and Myles Happ running the pottery, while Ros and Erl oversee the winery and vineyard.

After ten years teaching Erl used his long service break to complete the pottery, gallery and their new home. He converted a brick-making pug mill to make the sun-dried mud bricks, incorporating old telegraph poles and cross-arms from the Busselton-Wonnerup section of the old railway. He gave up teaching, the first vines were planted in 1978 and the winery built in 1980. Ros practiced for her higher-grade piano exams and finally passed the AMusA in piano performance while looking after their three young children and giving piano lessons.

In the early 1980s, establishing their business was a seven day a week operation, and a huge gamble. The pottery and winery both flourished, despite being off the beaten track up a 5 km gravel road, and quite 'out of the way' in those days. Other potters spent time at Happs, including Ian Dowling, who went on to establish Margaret River Pottery, and Gary Nichols, who then had Cowaramup Pottery for many years. The children made their own creations, and helped out with jobs such as cleaning shelves and labelling pots, so it was not surprising that eldest son Myles took up the reins, developing his own potting styles and taking over

The Pug-mill used to make the mud bricks for Happs' building management of the pottery and gallery with his wife, Jacquie, in 1999.

Erl at 67 is still passionately involved with wine, mainly in the development of the Three Hills Vineyard at Karridale where he grows 30 grape varieties and where, he says, the cooler climate results in richer and more intense flavours, so producing some special wines of which only the best are released under the Three Hills label. He is a climate sceptic who writes a blog where he explains how he believes natural factors are responsible for climate change.

Happs offer a wide range of wine styles, including the

A section of the pottery gallery

production of preservative free wines. They were the first Margaret River winery to make a rosé style wine they named 'Fuchsia'. This has been incredibly popular and many other wineries have followed suit. Their slightly sweet rosé style often appeals to first time wine drinkers, who may then move on to enjoy drier white and red wines in the future. Recently a white variant has been added.

Myles Happ sums up the unique family combination of pottery and vineyard with this quote from his website: "I am an artist in clay; my father is an artist in wine".

Happs colourful courtyard garden

HAY SHED HILL

Established: 1973

Yes, the first wines from this property were indeed made in a hayshed! The land was originally part of a large dairy farm, turned into a vineyard in the early 1970s when the wine industry in Margaret River was in its infancy. In those days it was called Sussex Vale, but received its new name from owners Liz and Barry Morrison, who bought it in 1989, and undertook a major rejuvenation of the property. Hay forks lying around from the old farm inspired the wine label, and the cellar door and winery were redesigned in 1992 by local architect, Chris Willcox, to compliment the existing buildings, especially the old hayshed, which was a local landmark when the farm was a dairy.

After a period from 2000 to 2006 when it was under corporate ownership, Hay Shed Hill was purchased by a small group of friends, including Leith Pavlinovich and winemaker, Michael Kerrigan, who now live on site. Michael started his career as a radiographer, but found his true talent as a winemaker, honing his skills at Howard Park where he became chief winemaker in 1999. The owners now proudly assert on the winery website that "winemakers have bought back the farm", and they are excited to be working with the mature vines from those early plantings, that, in their words, were " … the right varieties [planted] on the right slopes with the right soils".

Though the vineyard and winery operation at Hay Shed Hill is a highly professional one, the atmosphere is friendly and unpretentious, a relaxed destination for groups, and a welcoming one for families. The Deli Café menu announces "Food to Share" but that does not

Kids, dogs & chooks playing Please take care

detract from the quality of the items on offer. As befitting a former dairy farm, the café specializes in cheeses, boasting a spectacular international range. The cheeses are also available for purchase from the counter.

And what about the label on the 'Pitchfork' Series of wines? Well, the winemaker could perhaps be seen as a puppeteer who merely pulls the strings in the winemaking process. One way or another though, they're devilishly good wines!

A spectacular range of international cheeses to choose from

A topiary H and hayforks are a feature in the garden

HEYDON ESTATE

Established: 1988

Heydon Estate is located within the Wilyabrup Valley of the Margaret River appellation, with immediate neighbours of Vasse Felix and Cullen, where the first vines were planted in what was to become one of the great and iconic regions of new world wine. Their address, Tom Cullity Drive, is in recognition of one of these great pioneers, Dr Tom Cullity, who planted the first vines of Vasse Felix.

Whilst not quite as old, the first vines of Heydon Estate were planted in 1988, when the property was known as Arlewood Estate. George and Mary Heydon along with four partners purchased Arlewood in 1999, but following a restructure a few years later, the Heydons retained the property with these old vines, with a view to producing small quantities of iconic, single vineyard wines.

Heydon Estate was born!

Several wineries in the area have sporting associations, surfing being a favourite. Heydon Estate is all about cricket! George is, as Mary puts it, a 'Cricket Tragic'! He is passionate about the game, a fact that becomes clear as you enter the winery. It is full of fascinating cricket memorabilia. There is a bat signed by Don Bradman and other cricketing 'greats', a painting commemorating the Doug Walters '*Six*' – visit the winery to hear the story of this famous occasion – and a bust of the early pioneer of the game and reputed charlatan, *The Doc*, WG Grace. Just outside the cellar door is a sculpture of cricket bat, stumps, and cap, and

W G Grace

of course the wine labels continue the theme: the Cabernet Sauvignon is 'WG Grace', Chardonnay is 'The Willow', Shiraz is 'The Sledge' and Botrytis Semillon is 'The Urn'.

Growing grapes and making wine at Heydon Estate is not all fun and games though. Indeed George is as passionate about wine as he is about cricket, and both he and Mary work very hard to ensure that they follow best practices. The vineyard is carefully managed using traditional, organic and biodynamic principles, preserving soil health and vibrancy, and allowing the site to express its special *terroir*. The wines are bottle aged for a number of years before release, in keeping with the business philosophy to produce the finest wines possible. Production is small – 1500 cases – and initially, the Heydons did much of the work themselves, but with two boys at high school, and George continuing to work at his dental practice in nearby Margaret River four days a week, they do now have some help. However, George is still very involved with the winemaking process having studied viticulture and winemaking at post-graduate level at the University of Western Australia.

Mary came to Australia from Cork in Ireland in 1987, and amongst her travels, what better destination than the Americas Cup Yacht Race in Fremantle that year. George had come out from England somewhat earlier with his parents; his father's family had had a long-term connection with Australia, having arrived as free settlers in the eighteen thirties. They met soon after Mary arrived, and 25 years later, she is still here! George and Mary share another passion for mountain trekking and climbing. There isn't much time these days to get away to high places, though they do manage regular family ski trips. However, living in Australia's South West with its healthy and uncluttered lifestyle more than compensates for the absence of mountains. Mary is also a keen runner, and has won quite a few races, including the Perth Marathon and City to Surf, as well as several overseas events – Mary's best time for a marathon is 2 hours 45 minutes. It's a bit different around the bush tracks on Heydon Estate, but 110 acres still provides scope to keep her very fit. The sprint between the house and cellar door is usually covered several times a day!

The entrance to Heydon Estate is a long 1.3 km meandering driveway, following the creek-line and planted with 150 Liquid Ambers, which give way to native woodland full of wildflowers and birds as you near the cellar door.

The drive in, whilst itself stunning, is only the entrée to a most pleasurable Cellar Door experience, where wines are sampled in a relaxed atmosphere out of finest Reidel glassware.

The Ashes, illustrated here with birds and flowers from the woodland on the property

HOWARD PARK WINES

Howard Park Wines Established: 1986
Leston Vineyard Established: 1996

On entering Howard Park from either Miamup or Juniper Road, the meandering driveway lined with plane trees draws you in gently and allows you to slow your pace, relax and absorb the peace and harmony of your surroundings. This design is a central element in the Feng Shui philosophy that underpins everything about Amy and Jeff Burch's Leston Vineyard at Margaret River. This vineyard was named in honour of Jeff's father, Leston. Howard Park's first vineyard and winery was established on the south coast of Western Australia near Denmark. After planting the vineyard at Margaret River, the winery and cellar door here was built in 2000. Amy was the driving force behind construction. She drew on her Chinese heritage, engaging Feng Shui consultants Professor Cheng Juan Jun and Adriana Fernandes-Goncalves to create a building that would, she says, be built to grow old rather than be built "olde".

The winery and cellar door itself is situated on the highest point of the property. It commands sweeping views over the vineyard, and is aligned 2.5 degrees west of magnetic north, an orientation meant to bring good fortune. The building is constructed of contrasting materials, concrete and wood, stainless steel and large areas of glass that lets in plenty of light for the comfort of workers and visitors alike. Interior shapes are soft and rounded. The tasting area is spacious, allowing visitors plenty of room to take in their surroundings, and to feel relaxed and at home before tasting the wines. The bar itself is long, giving ample space for groups to enjoy their tastings without feeling crowded. Large wooden doors on the western side are perfectly placed to frame the shadows from the trees outside that fall on the polished floor in the late afternoon, and West Australian artist, Andrew Carter's painting, 'Howard Park Trees' on the opposite wall brings the outside environment into the interior, complete with its falling leaves.

Purple Swamphen

In the garden the colours of the flowers are predominantly warm reds and yellows, offsetting the cool concrete. The placement of water is also important. The pool is stocked with goldfish and koi, red and yellow, initially with an odd number and one black one for good luck. It can be enjoyed from the outside, but equally well from inside through the large glass windows beside the children's play area.

Leston Vineyard is managed to protect the environment, using organic and biodynamic farming principles, recycling, careful water management and other environmentally friendly measures. Amy and Jeff have also preserved as a bird sanctuary the wetland area that surrounds the Wilyabrup Brook near the old settlers' cottage. Flocks of both White and Straw-necked Ibis regularly roost in the trees here, and ducks and coots breed on the lake. Purple Swamphens clamber through the reeds, and many species of small birds inhabit the surrounding bushland.

Over the Chinese New Year period, visitors buying wine at Howard Park are given gifts of oranges, their round shape and warm colour signifying generosity and happiness, from a fat and bountiful land.

Chinese New Year is always celebrated at Howard Park

HOWLING WOLVES

Established: 1998

This was the date that the winery was built at Harmans Ridge. It was initially intended to be a contract winery, whose business was simply to make wine for small grape growers around the region. The wolves really started howling in 2002, however, when directors Damian Knowles, Vaughan Sutherland and Allan Waters decided to combine their knowledge and resources to create their own wines, made under the banner of the Howling Wolves Wine Group, a name inspired by one of their favourite African-American Blues artists, Howling Wolf. His music bursts out of the Howling Wolves website (it's a 'howler' of a site – have a look and a listen!), and no doubt helps the work along in the winery, especially during the busy days of vintage. The passion for music here goes further, however, as Howling Wolves sponsor a number of Australian music awards, as well as the Southbound Music Festival in Busselton.

No wonder the cow that graced the cellar door veranda throughout Margaret River's Cow Parade event in 2010 depicted famous country singers. Local artist, Sue Sowerby, designed this cow. She was called 'Cow-n-tree Moosic' – spoken with a (United States) country drawl! The resident corrugated cows had been howling for a year or two before this

though and, of course, the nearby town of Cowaramup, 'Cowtown' to local residents, prompted the 'Mootown' bottle label.

Howling Wolves have a strong export market to Asia where there is a growing appreciation and demand for Australian wines. They have an innovative project underway in India. A winery has been purchased and a vineyard planted in the hills behind Mumbai, where the climate is much cooler than down on the coastal plain. About 40 local people are employed and it is hoped that the business will help to boost the economy of their villages. Allan Waters loves the food and culture of India, and what better excuse would he need to visit India every so often in order to check on progress.

Stretching down the western side of India, south of Mumbai, are the Western Ghats, high mountains that, in parts, are still wild and remote. Who knows, there may yet be some real wolves out there, howling in the hills – or perhaps it is tigers that can be heard roaring ….

Tin cows howling at the moon

ISLAND BROOK ESTATE

Established: 1985

Island Brook Estate commenced life as part of a larger landholding that was mainly used for grazing and dairy farming. It was divided into smaller 40 hectare lots in the early 1980s, one of which became the vineyard and winery of Island Brook. The stream that gives the Estate its name meanders through the property, eventually flowing into the Carbunup River and into Geographe Bay. Several small islands are found along its course, two of these being on the Island Brook Estate property.

Visitors to the area in the 80s and 90s may remember the rammed earth maze that was built at Island Brook by a previous owner. This was dismantled, but in 2001 the winery gained a new landmark in the form of the red 1943 International KB 5 ton winery truck. This distinctive icon was owned originally by Stonyfell Wines in South Australia. It was used for general deliveries and later for promotional work for Stonyfell and then for the Arkaba Hotel, Adelaide, that acquired it in 1992. It was brought to Western Australia in 1999 where it was fully restored, licensed for the road, and driven down to Island Brook. The restoration included the fitting of a 5.7 litre motor with a T Bar automatic

Island Brook

transmission. The truck is still operational, though most of the time it now graces the entrance to the winery with its load of four wine barrels.

Island Brook Estate has had several owners. Having owned a house in the area for some time, and looking for a change Paul and Betty Zorzi bought Island Brook in 2006. They had thought long term of the possibilities of subdividing, but that all changed after living on the property. With a love of wine, and wanting to learn all they could about the wine industry, they set about rejuvenating the cellar door and chalets. They pride themselves on the appearance of the property and the wines they are now producing, and with a lot of care have more than doubled the production. Paul's parents had come to Western Australia from Northern Italy in 1950, when he was 12 months old, and he remembers helping his father make wine in the backyard shed in Osborne Park, so wine was definitely in the blood! With lots of help and encouragement from neighbours, and with a full-time viticulturist employed for a time to oversee the upgrade of the vineyard, Paul and Betty were soon fully involved in the wine industry.

Betty looks after the cellar door and chalet bookings, and Paul now manages the vineyard, but after completing his WSET (Wine and Spirits Education Trust) Sommeliers Course at Margaret River TAFE last year, he can often be found in the tasting room as well, where he loves to give visitors an in-depth tasting of all his wines. As well as the vineyard and winery, Island Brook has three comfortable chalets for holiday rental, tucked away amongst lovely Jarrah bushland on the western side of the winery. Nowadays there is certainly no shortage of things to keep the Zorzis busy! They say the best thing about this property is the amazing people they get to meet and have become friends with, both with the wine tasting and chalets.

The iconic red truck with an Australian Magpie

KNOTTING HILL ESTATE

Established: 1997

Brian Gould purchased the property at Knotting Hill in 1996. Growing a vineyard was the perfect lifestyle change that he and his son Michael wished for, after many years of farming wheat and sheep near Wongan Hills. As farmers, they were well used to tying knots, but they certainly got plenty of practice with the thousands of figure eight knots that were needed to tie the wires of the vine trellising. As they laboured up and down the hillside on the property, the name for their enterprise came to them in a flash!

Brian, Michael and farm dog Max off to work (left).

Silver Perch (right)

How to tie the Knotting Hill trellis knot

Knotting Hill's beautiful lake in front of the cellar door building holds a secret. It is stocked with marron and Silver Perch, and the winery, that usually just serves Platters and Tapas to compliment their wines, currently hosts a popular 'Marron Festival' over the Foundation Day June long weekend, allowing visitors to enjoy the produce of the lake. Many landholders keep marron, a fresh-water crayfish unique to the South West of WA, in their dams in order to enjoy a tasty feed now and again. Keeping them there is tricky, as they do like to wander and have been known to 'walk' several kilometres in search of more salubrious accommodation. It is also quite a long-term investment as they can take 3 to 5 years to grow large enough to harvest.

Silver Perch are native to the Murray-Darling River system in South-eastern Australia, but are a popular fish in farm dams in WA. They are a good fish to have in the lake at Knotting Hill, as they seem to live harmoniously with the marron, although in the wild they do eat yabbies and shrimp. Wild populations are now in serious decline due to deteriorating conditions in the river systems, and to competition from introduced carp, but in the Knotting Hill Lake they seem to be thriving and breeding successfully. The Silver Perch, which darken to bronze as they age, are a popular attraction for visitors to the winery, who are able to enjoy watching and feeding them from the deck in front of the cellar door.

The architecturally designed cellar door, opened in 2005, is a light, airy building with glass panels to the ceiling all along the north side, to take full advantage of the lake view and the winter sun. The huge windows, sinuous curve of the roofline, and pale stone walls combine to make this a spectacular venue for functions, and the delightful bridge entry makes Knotting Hill an ideal bridal setting. Or 'Why Not?' simply visit and enjoy the atmosphere with a cheese platter and a delicious glass of wine.

LAMONTS, MARGARET RIVER

Established: 2001

It is hard to imagine a more perfect setting in which to match great food and wine than the cellar door and restaurant at Lamonts near Yallingup. Overlooking a picturesque lake, with Gunyulgup Gallery nearby, this makes an ideal venue for a romantic occasion or just lunch with friends.

Margaret River is renowned for its superb produce as well as its world-class wines, with venison, marron, cheeses, olives, avocados, and a growing list of other delectable goodies produced in the area. These regularly find their way onto the menu at Lamonts. The marron lunch shown here is Lamonts' signature dish and a special South West treat. Marron, or fresh-water crayfish, are native to the rivers and streams of the South West of Western Australia, and are eagerly sought by locals in the short open season when fishing is allowed during

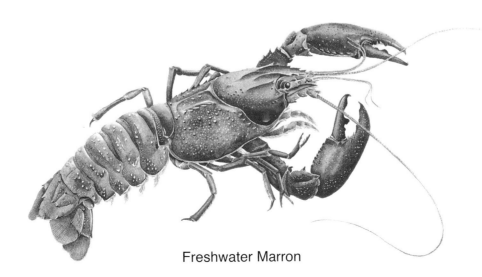

Freshwater Marron

January and February. There is even a particular species, the Hairy Marron, found only in the Margaret River catchment, but this one is unlikely to turn up on your dinner table, as it is unfortunately now very uncommon.

Kate Lamont grew up with food and wine. Her grandfather was Jack Mann, winemaker at Houghtons Winery for 51 vintages, and her parents, Corin and Neil, established Lamonts in the Swan Valley in the 1970s. After a stint of teaching, and studying wine making, she found that her niche was in business in the hospitality industry. With her sister, Fiona, they proudly opened their Margaret River cellar door and restaurant in 2001. They also operate the 8000 case production family winery in the Swan Valley that draws grapes from across the South West,

as well as a restaurant in Bishops House in the Perth CBD, and a wine store and tapas bar in Cottesloe.

Kate became one of Western Australia's most successful chefs, has written several best-selling cookery books, and contributes regularly to magazines and radio programs.

She won the "Business Owners Award" in the WA Telstra Business Woman of the Year Awards in 1996, and has served on many Government boards and committees, becoming especially involved with wine tourism. She was appointed to Tourism WA's Board of Commissioners in 2004, and became Chairman for a five-year term in 2006.

Her personal motto is "Never, never, never, never give up!"

Lamonts signature dish

LAURANCE WINES

Garden of Eden tree

Established: 2001

The cellar door at Laurance Wines is a feast for the eyes. As you walk into the tasting area, the magnificence of the interior is breathtaking, with its huge wooden supporting beams made of ironbark, a wood too heavy to float. These were sourced from the old Woolloomooloo Jetty in Sydney; Dianne Laurance bought them all when the jetty was dismantled. The highly polished floor is the result of layer upon layer of glaze over concrete.

The winery and garden are entirely Dianne's creation, which is evident from the loving attention to detail and the impressive display of artworks both inside and outside the building. These include the wineglass chandeliers that hang in the entrance hall, and an amazing sculpted head of Murano Glass by Cuban artist, Alfredo Sosabravo, that greets you as you come in. Called 'La Amiga de los Animales' it is one of only nine that were made. A large birdbath surrounded by Palm Cockatoos in the garden is dedicated to the memory of Queensland naturalist, Steve Irwin.

This winery is best known, however, for its iconic sculpture, known variously as The Diver, Lady of the Lake, the Golden Lady, or the 'Chick on a Stick' – "I initiated that name!" Dianne says with a twinkle in her eye. Her real title is 'Free as a

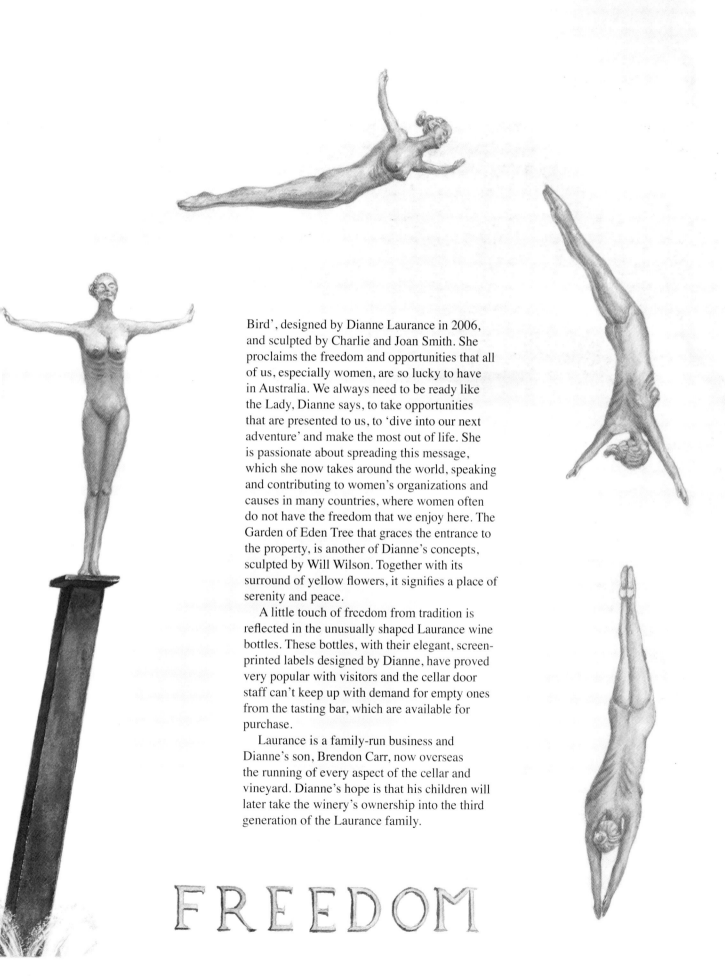

Bird', designed by Dianne Laurance in 2006, and sculpted by Charlie and Joan Smith. She proclaims the freedom and opportunities that all of us, especially women, are so lucky to have in Australia. We always need to be ready like the Lady, Dianne says, to take opportunities that are presented to us, to 'dive into our next adventure' and make the most out of life. She is passionate about spreading this message, which she now takes around the world, speaking and contributing to women's organizations and causes in many countries, where women often do not have the freedom that we enjoy here. The Garden of Eden Tree that graces the entrance to the property, is another of Dianne's concepts, sculpted by Will Wilson. Together with its surround of yellow flowers, it signifies a place of serenity and peace.

A little touch of freedom from tradition is reflected in the unusually shaped Laurance wine bottles. These bottles, with their elegant, screen-printed labels designed by Dianne, have proved very popular with visitors and the cellar door staff can't keep up with demand for empty ones from the tasting bar, which are available for purchase.

Laurance is a family-run business and Dianne's son, Brendon Carr, now oversees the running of every aspect of the cellar and vineyard. Dianne's hope is that his children will later take the winery's ownership into the third generation of the Laurance family.

FREEDOM

LEEUWIN ESTATE

Established: 1975

Leeuwin is a name that appears frequently around the south west corner of the State. It derives from the Dutch East India Company ship of that name, and means 'Lioness'. The Leeuwin visited the south west coast in the 1620s. The ship was on its way to Batavia in the colony of the East Indies but as often happened, it strayed too far south on the journey and encountered the 'Leeuwin Land' or 'Great Southland' as Australia was then known. The coast between Point Nuyts and Hamelin Bay was explored and charted before the ship turned north to Batavia. A 17th century clog was discovered near Augusta in the 1930s, suggesting that some of the sailors from that, or other Dutch ships, may have come ashore. However, it was much later that Englishman, Matthew Flinders, actually named Cape Leeuwin during his voyage of discovery around the continent in 1801.

Leeuwin Estate, though established a little later than the initial pioneers, still belongs to the first generation of wineries in the Margaret River Wine Region. Renowned Californian winemaker, Robert Mondavi, identified the Leeuwin Estate site as having great potential for fine varietal wines, and encouraged and advised founders, Tricia and Denis Horgan, in its transformation from cattle farm to 'State of the Art' vineyard and winery.

The Horgans led the way in embracing the concept of 'Wine Tourism' in the region. Leeuwin's impressive winery building

and restaurant opened in 1978 and soon became a magnet for visitors. The sweeping curve of Boodjidup Brook, with its floodlit backdrop of Karri trees, imparted a fairytale-like atmosphere to Saturday night dining. The long dining tables, crafted from some of the property's original pine trees by farm manager, Henry Kowalski, and the fine collection of paintings showcased on the labels of the 'Art Series' wines from 1980, added to the experience.

The first of the famous Leeuwin Concerts was held in February 1985. The audience enjoyed picnics on the grass and the London Philharmonic Orchestra gave a stirring performance, despite the challenges of keeping instruments in tune on one of the hottest Margaret River afternoons on record. Some members of the orchestra were a little sunburnt after a trip to the beach and the kookaburras tried hard to upstage the performance, but nevertheless the concert was a resounding success.

After the initial concert, the innovative 'shell' stage was designed and this became a hallmark of future performances that have included such well-known names as Dionne Warwick, Ray Charles, Sting and Shirley Bassey. The shell gave the artists shelter from the weather, which can be fickle in Margaret River even at the height of summer. When Tricia Horgan collected Tom Jones from Margaret River airstrip for his concert, it had been pouring with rain all day. As she drove him to the winery a tiny patch of blue appeared in the sky – right above the concert shell so all will be well, Tricia joked to Tom. Sure enough when they arrived, it was still there, immediately above the stage, and the evening was wonderful! Another year, after much deliberation, the concert went ahead despite a backdrop of fine, misty drizzle. The audience bravely donned their ponchos, and Dame Kiri Te Kanawa and James Galway, very mindful of the people's discomfort, performed one of the most memorable Leeuwin Concerts ever.

Leeuwin Estate also hosts an Australia Day family concert each year, and sometimes others throughout the summer. Each is an occasion for up to 6000 devotees to meet friends and share picnics and wine on the lawn, to enjoy the relaxed atmosphere, and listen to sublime music as the sun goes down.

Kookaburras join concerts
at dusk with a good laugh

Dame Kiri Te Kanawa performing at Leeuwin Estate

LENTON BRAE ESTATE

Established: 1982

The magnificent winery building at Lenton Brae is a proud achievement for designer and owner, Bruce Tomlinson. Bruce was an architect and town-planning consultant who had previously spent much time working in the North West, one of his major projects being the original plan for the townsite of Karratha. He had also designed many of the public buildings there.

After moving south, Bruce and wife, Jeanette, had a change in direction and established Lenton Brae in the early 1980s. The idea had been planted during a conversation with Bill Pannell of Moss Wood Estate, for whom Bruce was advising on the planning requirements for subdividing his property. Bill suggested that the soils of one of his subdivisions were excellent and equal to those of the Moss Wood vineyard, so Bruce decided to buy it and try his hand at viticulture. After planting the vineyard, the rammed earth winery was finally finished in 1989.

The winery has a superb leadlight window by Perth artist, Heather Jones, entitled 'Sunlight through Canopy'. It also features a viewing platform through which visitors can observe the winery operations and enjoy the sweeping view over the Wilyabrup Valley. However, perhaps its most

'Sunlight through Canopy'

intriguing aspect is the pair of bell towers at either end of the building. The name 'Lenton Brae' commemorates the Tomlinsons' British forebears, Lenton being the name of the chapel district near Nottingham from whence the family emigrated in 1884, and 'brae' is the Scots term for a little hill (several grandparents had come originally from Scotland).

The Tomlinson family held a '100th year Anniversary of Arrival at Fremantle' celebration in 1984, soon after the establishment of the vineyard. Three years later, a double tragedy ensued when two close family members died suddenly, and when the winery was built, the family decided to have the bells foundered in their memory. Five bells were made to ring on a pentatonic scale. This proved to be only half the challenge as engineering a striking mechanism was also quite a task. However, with the help of friends and family, the bells were made to peal and for several years they rang out over the vines for a minute at midday each day. Unfortunately, a few years ago, it became evident to those with a musical ear that the bells needed re-tuning, and they are currently residing at the Department of Engineering Acoustics at the University of WA. Hopefully, it won't be too long before the Lenton Brae Bells are heard again across the Wilyabrup Valley.

Jeanette purchased the interesting old hand pump at the front of the building from a friend's antique shop. It is at least 100 years old, and comes from the Beaune District of Burgundy in France. As their automatic pumps whirr in the winery today, moving the wine from tank to tank, or tank to barrel, Jeanette often thinks about what a hard job it must have been in the old days, when only hand pumps such as this were available.

The old hand pump

MARRI WOOD PARK

Established: 1993

Marri Wood Park was established in 1993, but it wasn't until 11 years later in 2004 that owners Lisa and Julian Wright were able to move to Yallingup and take over the running of the vineyard.

After watching the precautions that were necessary when spraying the vines with chemicals – full protective clothing, breathing apparatus, air-conditioned vehicles – they were horrified, and soon became committed to the principles of biodynamic farming, which aims to restore the health of the soil using a holistic approach, with only natural fertilizers and special preparations. Manure for the vines comes from the cattle, sheep and chickens that are now an integral part of the farm. The noisy flock of guinea fowl is also a very important part of the operation, keeping the grasshoppers and other insect pests in check. They are supposed to patrol the vineyard of course, though they are often on hand to greet visitors.

The guinea fowl feature on the labels of Marri Wood Park's 'Guinea Run' range of wines in a delightful cartoon by the late Paul Rigby. The 'Marri' and 'Grandis' wines celebrate two of our local trees, Marri or Red Gum, *Corymbia calophylla*, and Bull Banksia, *Banksia grandis*, both of which are common in the surrounding bushland. Marri flowers in late summer and autumn, and is a valuable food source for native birds such as silvereyes and parrots, when not much else is available.

Vignerons cross their fingers each year that the Marri's flowering coincides with the ripening grapes, as the birds do prefer their natural Marri flower food if it is available.

The stout golden flower spikes of the Bull Banksia that develop in spring and summer, give mature trees the appearance of spreading candelabras. This tree was one of the

Guinea Fowl

most useful to the indigenous people of the area – the mature woody cones were used as firesticks to carry lighted coals from camp to camp, and the nectar from flowers was eaten, as were the grubs that burrowed into the flower spikes; but most enjoyed was a beverage made by soaking the flowers in water to produce a sweet drink that would often be left to ferment rather like mead. It sometimes provided a focus for social gatherings, and could be quite potent if drunk in large quantities.

The tradition continues at Marri Wood Park, and the cellar door has a delightful shady garden overlooking the vines, where visitors can enjoy a bottle of wine with a selection of local organic and biodynamic cheeses, dried fruits and Yallingup bread.

Guinea Run

Two distinct varieties, the dark and the more unusual pale colour, of Guinea Fowl, resting on the restored light spring trap outside the cellar door

McHenry Hohnen Vintners[†]

Established: 2004

It is a well-known fact that horses and pigs don't get along. Sandy Hohnen's mare certainly did not appreciate the pigs when they first arrived on their McLeod Creek farm. It was a wild, windy day and the startled horse bolted, throwing Sandy to the ground, but luckily injuring only her pride. After this, she was excused from feeding the new arrivals! She does, however, now juggle her passion for riding with helping out one or two days a week in the McHenry Hohnen farm shop and cellar door that opened in April 2010.

David and Sandy Hohnen established Cape Mentelle vineyard and winery in the 1970s, and developed it into one of Margaret River's most iconic wineries. They changed direction in 2003, establishing a new farming venture in which they would raise pigs and sheep for the table, as well as continuing to grow vines. The sheep are often seen amongst the vines, where they fertilize the soil and keep the weeds at bay. David now grows 18 different types of grape, including many lesser-known varieties, as well as the traditional tried and tested ones. David's philosophy in working the land is what he calls 'Great-grandpa's Farming', based on common sense principles of farming, in which 'the soil and its organisms, along with plants, insects and animals, can coexist in a thriving equilibrium'.

The site for the cellar door, farm shop and café at McHenry Hohnen is on land originally owned by Sandy's mother. Behind the buildings, this block stretches over the hill to a sunny north-facing vineyard that slopes down to the banks of the Margaret River. This vineyard and one on the McLeod Creek farm, together with two vineyards owned by Sandy's brother, Murray McHenry, produce the fruit for McHenry Hohnen wines. The whole enterprise is very much a family affair. David is in charge of the vineyard and the farm, while daughter, Freya with her partner, Ryan Walsh, make the wine. Freya also oversees the farm shop and cellar door. The cosy patio café, warmed in winter by huge pottery braziers, and featuring delectable home-cooked produce with a French flair, completes this unique family business.

The pigs bred on the farm are Tamworth variety. These are large attractive ginger pigs with straight ears. They are excellent mothers who sit down carefully and never roll on their piglets. Big Red, illustrated here, is the farm favourite. Over her life she has had approximately 180 piglets. She reminds Patricia of the line from a well-known poem, "There in a wood a piggywig stood _____".

A grove of French Oak trees provides the pigs with large acorns, their favourite food. Truffles are not grown here because the pigs would find and eat them.

† At the time of writing it was likely that the name of this establishment would change. Check http://www.capetocape.8m.com for updates

French Oak acorns

Big Red and her spotty piglets

McLeod Creek Wines

Established: 1999

Erminio (Mario) Iannarelli grew up in Italy, in a little village situated between Rome and Naples called Belmonte Castello. He then lived in Switzerland and later Germany for a while before moving to Cornwall in England. As well as Italian, Mario speaks fluent French and English, but says he couldn't get his head around the German language. Always working in the hospitality industry he travelled to London, but after a while decided to go to Jersey in the Channel Islands, where he met his wife, Jenny, and stayed for seven years.

Jenny and Mario moved to Perth, Australia, in 1970, and ran a restaurant in Claremont for 20 years named Trattoria La Cappaninna. Have a look at the fine oak table in the tasting room at McLeod Creek. It came from a mature oak tree on the property next door to the Claremont restaurant. Mario was horrified one day to see this being chopped down and loaded onto a truck destined for the rubbish tip. He persuaded the workers to tip it over the fence instead!

Feeling the need for land and the fresh air of the country again after all those years, they looked for a property in the Margaret River area and found the farm at McLeod Creek. It had nothing but pasture, a winter creek and some beautiful granite outcrops, an empty slate on which Mario could weave his magic! And a magical transformation it has been. As well as the flourishing vineyard, there are chickens and ducks, long raised beds of organically grown vegetables, garlic and herbs. In the blossoming fruit orchard there are the usual apples, pears, plums, apricots, oranges, but also a few surprises: an Irish strawberry tree, a persimmon, a guava, a bay tree and two kinds of limes. But Mario's favourites are two rows of various varieties of fig tree, the fruits of which are in great demand from local restaurants.

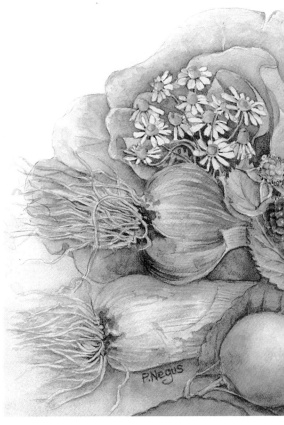

P.Negus

McLeod Creek fig chutney is in the pipeline at the time of writing.

Mario tends his produce with loving care usually with Jade, the pet parrot, perched on his shoulder. Beware, Jade is very friendly towards men, but hates women! Mario insists there is still much work to be done on his property. He plans to grow avocados in the winter creek valley, and more fruit trees are lined up ready for planting. How does he find all his energy, at an age when most people would be putting their feet up, travelling the continent or relaxing on cruises? He reckons chia seeds are the answer. Chia seeds were first used as food as early as 3500 BC and were one of the main dietary components of the Aztecs. They are particularly rich in omega-3 fatty acids, and are now being embraced by the western world as a 'superfood'. Mario Iannarelli would certainly agree with that.

The photo shows 40 year-old Grappa and Chianti bottles from Mario's collection, on display in the tasting area.

Mario and Jade with some of his home-grown produce

MINOT WINES

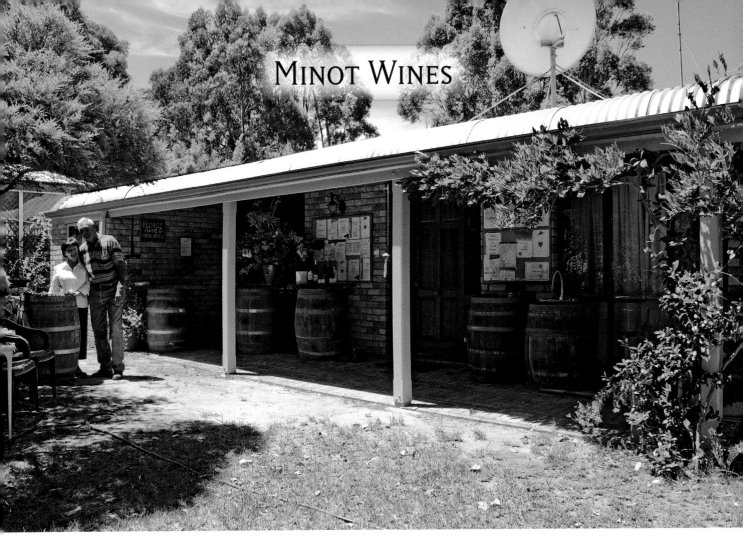

Established: 1993

Ken and Madeleine Miles established Minot Vineyard in 1993, following their arrival in Margaret River from the Western Australian wheatbelt town of Coorow, where they had operated a 4,800 acre wheat and sheep farm. So it was – from wheat to wine! 10 acres of vines would be a piece of cake, they thought. Reality proved a bit different. Growing the vines and marketing the wine turned out to be two full-time jobs, and a steep learning curve for them both!

The name 'Minot' originates with a family who owned a small 15th century chateau, 'Le Petit Chateau', in the village of Azay-sur-Indre, France, in the early part of the 20th century. Madeleine is French-born and comes from this little village that is near Tours in the Loire Valley. Her parents enjoyed a long association with the Minot family, and from her childhood she remembers many stories about the family and the chateau household. It was rumoured, for instance, that after abdicating the English Throne, Edward VIII and Mrs. Wallace Simpson holidayed quietly there with their friends, the Minots, away from the prying eyes of the Press.

Madame Minot was famous throughout the region for her ménage of poodles that were chauffeured to major dog shows across Europe, always accompanied by Madame, with valet, maid and, of course, the chauffeur. The dogs won many awards, not without drama on occasion, as when a scratch was discovered on the nose of prize poodle 'Gregoire' just before a prestigious championship event in Monaco. Disaster was averted by the quick-thinking chauffeur and, with a dab of boot polish to the nose, 'Gregoire' won the class: Championnat de Beaute Monegasque. All breathed a sigh of relief, Madame Minot was happy, and the chateau household slept well again.

Flanders Poppies

The Minot family left France for Switzerland just before the outbreak of World War II and the chateau remained empty. Its grounds and cellars, however, played a part in the rescue of Allied airmen who were smuggled across the country from town to town on moonless nights by members of the French Resistance. They would be hidden at the chateau, or in neighbouring farms, on their way to the French coast or to Spain, where, if lucky, they would find a boat to take them to England. Cryptic messages would sometimes be sent back to France via the Red Cross and later, when Madeleine was a child in Australia, she remembers her parents' silent tears of joy as they recalled such successful outcomes. The Flanders Poppy that grows wild in the Minot vineyard is a yearly reminder to Madeleine of those occasions. It is now depicted on one of the Minot labels.

The word 'Minot' reminds Ken and Madeleine of minnows, being very small fish in the big pond of the Margaret River Wine Industry. Today, however, they are proud of their small vineyard that now produces award-winning, premium quality wines from low-yielding vines. With a glass of fine Minot 'red' in his hand, Ken feels like a king in his chateau in the heart of the Margaret River region!

Madame Minot

Le Petit Chateau

PIERRO

Established: 1979

    The whimsical folk tale of Pierrot and Columbine is familiar to most European children, but probably not so well known to Australians. The part comic, part tragic character of Pierrot, together with Columbine, and Harlequin, has been part of European theatre culture for many generations. Poor Pierrot was hopelessly in love with Columbine and continually tried to woo her, but alas, his naive advances were always rebuffed, for she much preferred the dashing Harlequin. Pierrot is always portrayed as rather foolish, and is pictured with a tear in his eye as he pines away for his lost love. More recently, the story was the theme of a song by British folk group, The Seekers.

    When Mike Peterkin bought his plot of land in 1979, his friends and mentors considered him somewhat foolish, as the block was scrubby, rocky and steep sloping. He felt some affinity with his namesake – Pierrot, like Peterkin, means 'son of Peter' or 'son of the rock'. But the slopes were north facing, the Wilyabrup Brook flowed through the property, the Indian Ocean was just over the hill, and it was a wonderfully picturesque location. Cullen Wines was also 'only a stones' throw' away. This was important, as Mike had met Shelley Cullen, whom he later married, while winemaking for Kevin and Di Cullen, a short time before.

    The gruelling work of clearing those stones and undergrowth, and preparing the ground for vines took two years, undertaken while Mike was still working at his first profession as a medical doctor in Busselton. He then went against conventional wisdom of the time, planting high-density vines, in north-south oriented rows, and making limited use of irrigation. He also introduced blended styles to the region, Semillon Sauvignon Blanc in the whites, and Cabernet Merlot in the reds, in the days when single varietals were much more in vogue. These blends have proved themselves, however, and are now the pre-eminent styles of Margaret River. Mike Peterkin believes "just as Pierrot personifies life's intricacies and passions, Pierro wine is a wonderfully complex balance of sensual and fascinating elements".

Pierro was home for several years to the Willyabrup Descent[†]. In years of high rainfall, the Wilyabrup Brook can become a formidable torrent, and in the early 1980s an idea was hatched for a barrel race between Margaret River wineries down the short, but exacting stretch of water between Ribbon Vale vineyard and Pierro. The event was adopted with gusto, reputations were at stake, and wineries around the area put their best teams forward. The Descent was held after pruning each year, and at its peak, upwards of 200 people would line the banks of the brook to

PIERRO

COLUMBINE

watch the thrills and spills. It was a perilous affair however, and the dangers of losing a proportion the region's grape-growing and winemaking talent became greater with the increasing popularity of each year's race. As questions of liability insurance and potential litigation loomed, the event was eventually abandoned, and a small chapter in the history of the Margaret River Wine Region was closed. The lovely wooden and rammed earth cellar door at Pierro Winery, by contrast, remains well and truly open to visitors throughout the year.

[†]Alternative spelling

PREVELI WINES

Established: 1995

The little coastal settlement of Prevelly Park is, nowadays, best known for its world-class surf breaks. The Margaret River Masters Competition is a major event on the surfing calendar each March, and other surf and body-board championships are held through the year. More and more frequently, you can also watch the antics of kite-surfers and, usually in the afternoons, the wind-surfers take to the waves.

Back at the Prevelly Park Beach Resort and Liquor Store, you can indulge in that other favourite Margaret River pastime of wine tasting, as the store also doubles as the cellar door for Preveli Wines. The Home family have lived at Prevelly for three generations. Their vineyard is actually tucked away at Rosa Brook, 15 km inland from Margaret River, where the climate is more conducive to grape growing, but the Prevelly Store makes a classic venue where you can taste the wine and watch the surf at the same time. Preveli Wines also have a distinctively local label, designed by Prevelly Park artist and surfer, Mark Heussenstamm.

It was Geoff Edwards who originally developed the Prevelly Park settlement in the 1950s. He and his wife, Beryl, dreamt of starting a holiday resort somewhere in the South West, and after looking at sites in Albany and Denmark, they fell in love with the coast at the mouth of the Margaret River, where

Father Emmanuel Stamatiou
and Father Chris Stouris

a 100 acre block was available for sale. It took several years of hard work to establish the camping ground, caravan park and chalets, securing it as a holiday destination for the future. As well as doing all the building work, they had to promote this lonely place that no-one had heard of in those days, and on a trip back from the East pamphlets were dropped at all stops across the Nullarbor! Later Geoff and Beryl were able to subdivide the land to the south for house blocks, and the township was born.

The stark limestone landscape of this coast reminded Geoff very much of the settlement of Preveli on the Greek island of Crete, where he was amongst many Australian soldiers trying to evade capture by the Germans during the Second World War. The local people, especially the monks at the Preveli monastery, bravely hid the soldiers and helped them to escape, often at great cost to their own safety. Many were later executed by the Germans. In gratitude for their courageous help, Geoff named the little township Prevelly Park. In conjunction with the West Australian Greek community, he later built the Greek Orthodox chapel that stands on the hill as a memorial to the people of Preveli in Crete.

The Greek Orthodox chapel

REDGATE WINES

Established: 1977

There are a number of stories surrounding the name 'Redgate'. The one that inspired Bill Ullinger's choice of name for his winery told of a nearby property that, many years ago, had a reputation for making excellent 'Moonshine'. That property was named for its red gate, and Bill thought the same name would fit nicely with the alcoholic nature of his new enterprise.

Another legend involves the sign on the painted red gate across the original sand track leading from Caves Road down to Calgardup Beach. "Shut the bloody gate!" signalled a grazier's frustration with beachgoers as he tried to keep the cattle contained on his pastoral lease along the coast. Long before the Leeuwin-Naturaliste National Park was gazetted, through the first half of the 20th century, grazing rights on many of the coastal reserves were leased to local landholders. Wild steers, as well as domestic cattle, were brought from inland and from the north in summer, to take advantage of the greener pastures along the south west coast. The country was much more open then, but you can still see the remains of old fence lines in several places, now hidden amongst the dense bushland that has re-established since the cattle departed. The gate itself has long since gone, and the sand track is now a sealed road, but the beach became known as Redgate Beach, though many long-time locals still use the old name of Calgardup.

This beach saw high drama in December 1876, when a corvette, the Georgette, bringing supplies and settlers to Augusta from Perth, was shipwrecked just offshore. Grace Bussell and stockman, Sam Isaacs, were out mustering cattle along the Ridge, and seeing the vessel in difficulties, galloped down to the beach where they made repeated forays into the waves to assist the 60 or so passengers and crew. All were safely rescued and taken to shelter at the Bussell family home of Wallcliffe House.

Bill Ullinger and his son Paul founded Redgate Wines not long after the first wineries had been established in the region. Bill had been a Lancaster bomber pilot during World War II, and had an engineering business for 20 years after the war, but was lured to the new wine region of Margaret River to try his hand at growing grapes and making wine. Their first vintage was in 1981, and in 1982 Redgate won the Montgomery Trophy for the best Cabernet at the Adelaide Wine Show. They were off to a flying start.

The winery and cellar door sit on a steep hillside amongst some huge Marri trees, overlooking the picturesque Boodjidup Valley. It lies only 4 km from the coast and, on a sunny day, you can just see the ocean glinting between the hills.

Original Red Gate with flowering
Marri and male Scarlet Robin

Winery entrance with
female Scarlet Robin

ROSILY VINEYARD

Established: 1994

Rosily Vineyard is named after Comte François-Étienne de Rosily-Mesros (1748 – 1832), a French navigator and cartographer, who was intimately involved in the ongoing French explorations of Western Australia during the late 18th and early 19th centuries. Rosily himself made only one voyage to Terra Australis, on one of the earlier expeditions, in 1772, as an ensign on the 'Gros Ventre' commanded by Louis de St. Alouarn. He had started the voyage on the Gros Ventre's sister ship, the 'Fortune' commanded by Yves Joseph de Kerguelen-Trémarec, but had become separated whilst undertaking a survey of the newly discovered Kerguelen Island that, at the time, was mistakenly thought to be part of the great southern landmass that they were seeking. Kerguelen turned back to Mauritius, abandoning the unfortunate Rosily and his crew, who were luckily rescued later by Louis de St. Alouarn. The 'Gros Ventre' continued east until it encountered the south west coast of Australia at Cape Leeuwin, where Rosily made the first, but very accurate survey of Flinders Bay. They then sailed north to Shark Bay where Rosily made another accurate map of that section of coast. It was here, at Dirk Hartog Island, that St. Alouarn formally annexed Western Australia for France.

By the 1820s, Rosily had risen to the influential position of Director of the Hydrographic Office in Paris, and was one of the few who were enthusiastic about future French settlement in Western Australia. Although there had been several exploratory expeditions by the French, including the great scientific voyages of Baudin and Freycinet, 1801 – 03, no attempt had been made to colonize this new land. At that time France was embroiled in the Napoleonic Wars, and Western Australia was generally viewed as arid and inhospitable. However, France, like Britain, was experiencing an overcrowding problem in its gaols, and by the early 1820s Western Australia was seen as a potential French penal colony. Rosily and others championed this idea, and several expeditions were sent to make detailed surveys of the South West in preparation for establishing a settlement. The French activity alarmed the British enough to dispatch a contingent of men from their colony in New South Wales to occupy King George Sound in December 1826, and to claim the whole of Western Australia for Britain. The threat was averted, and the French turned their attention to New Zealand where they settled at Akaroa, near Christchurch, and to Tahiti and New Caledonia in the Pacific.

Rosily Vineyard uses the attractive French 'Fleur-de-lys' motif on its labels, as a reminder of the French connection that nearly was. The Fleur-de-lys, a stylised lily flower, is actually an ancient symbol with connections to many cultures. In early Christianity it symbolised the Holy Trinity and can be seen in carvings in many churches and cathedrals. It was a symbol of the French Monarchy, appearing on banners and flags until the French Revolution. It was also used to show North on early maps. More recently it became the main element in the logo of the International Scouting Movement, representing the threefold Scout Promise: Duty to God and Country, Duty to Self, Duty to Others.

What do vignerons and oenologists do when they are not growing grapes and making wine? Well, in Margaret River, many of them, including those at Rosily Vineyard, Mike Lemmes, Mick Scott and Sam Castleden, take advantage of the region's other famous attraction and surf the local breaks. One of the Rosily Vineyard wines, the 'Other Side of the Moon', takes

its name from a spectacular surf break near Cape Naturaliste. Continuing the sporting connection, one of Rosily Vineyard's directors, Ben Allan, has been a premier league footballer, winning Best and Fairest for Hawthorn in 1991, and later playing and coaching for the Fremantle Dockers. Though his career is now in marketing premium wines, including those of Rosily Vineyard, he maintains his connection with the Dockers, currently holding a position as Vice President on the Board of the Fremantle Football Club (2011).

Comte Francois de Rosily

SARACEN ESTATES

Saladin, the chivalrous knight

Established: 1996

The small island in the lake at Saracen Estates holds a secret. Take time when visiting the cellar door to walk across the footbridge to the island, where you will find the Temple of Wine, set amidst pretty gardens with a fabulous view back to Saracen Estates Winery and the Duckstein Brewery complex – a unique combination in the Margaret River region. The gazebo-like structure of the Wine Temple consists of six beautifully etched glass panels depicting the history of wine through the ages, beginning with the Neolithic period, and continuing through the Mesopotamian, Egyptian, Greek, Roman and Medieval eras. The illustrations are supported by detailed text on each period.

The Saracens were themselves an ancient group of people, living in the North West of the Arabian Peninsula. The term 'Saracen' is Greek in origin, derived from the Arabic word for Easterners, and they are referred to extensively in the writings of the Romans with whom they often came into conflict. Later, their great military leader, Saladin, a sultan of Egypt and Syria, led the Islamic opposition to the Third Crusade in the 12th Century. The Saracens were considered to be one of the world's most culturally and socially advanced races at the time, excelling in particular in art and mathematics. Saladin, himself, was highly educated and, despite his fierce struggle against the Crusades, achieved a great reputation in Europe as a chivalrous knight. The Saracens spread around the Mediterranean and conquered and settled in parts of Italy, including the Abruzzi Region, home to the Saraceni family, owners of Saracen Estates.

The family migrated to Australia after the Second World War, and from a small fine wine importation business, they expanded into commercial production of their own wines, and thence to development of the impressive Saracen Estates winery and cellar door. Maree Saraceni, in particular, has overseen the development of the facility. She has been especially keen to support local artisans. Local works, along with artwork and jewellery crafted by family members, as well as local jams and condiments, are displayed and sold at special Market Days that are held at various times of the year at the cellar door, along with other festivals at the venue.

Other features of the Saracen cellar door include the 'Wine Education Centre' and the collection of 'Guest Wines' from around the world, especially from Europe, that are available for sale. In an unusual move to showcase wines other than their own, the Saraceni family want to encourage visitors to expand their palates and compare their wines with what the rest of the world has to offer. In their words "It's all about learning".

The Temple of Wine

SWALLOWS WELCOME

Established: 1994

Chance has played a big part in the lives of Tim and Patricia Negus. Perhaps it's the same for everyone, but certainly it was a series of chance events that led Tim and Patricia to Margaret River, where Tim became a grape grower and winemaker and Patricia an illustrator of books.

Tim grew up in Somerset, England, and Patricia on a dairy farm in Cornwall. They met at Reading University where Tim was studying agriculture and Patricia science. They spent the first year of their married life in Trinidad, Tim studying tropical agriculture and Patricia teaching. They then moved to Zambia for three years, where their daughter, Sally, was born at Livingstone Hospital. Western Australia was the next stop, though it could just as easily have been Queensland or Fiji! They were posted to Narrogin in the wheatbelt, where Tim worked as an agricultural advisor for 26 years. Their son, Richard was born an Aussie at Narrogin Hospital. Patricia continued to teach until 1976, when she made a decision to start a new full-time career as an artist.

By chance, Patricia's sister, Mandy, settled with her family in Margaret River. She and Mark were building their own house, as many local residents were doing at the time. Tim thought 'If they can do it, we can too', not quite acknowledging the 20 years' difference in their ages! They found a block of 130 acres at East Witchcliffe, and spent frequent visits over

Digger, the camera-shy wine-dog

Welcome Swallow

growers, including his dentist while waiting for the anaesthetic to kick in! North Devon cattle were off the agenda! Tim opened his cellar door in 1998.

The name for their property, Swallows Welcome, came after one visit to the half-finished home when they found that a pair of Welcome Swallows had built their nest on top of the wall. It seemed very appropriate, as Tim and Patricia like to think that visitors are always welcome. It was also a good play on the word 'swallow' although at that time the wine had not yet been considered.

Patricia's art career has taken a sideways step since moving to Margaret River, after getting together with Jane Scott and Ray Forma to produce a number of walking and natural history books about the South West, under the banner of Cape to Cape Publishing. After she had painted 102 pictures of 502 Margaret River wildflowers for one of these books, Tim was anxious that she should keep this unique collection together, and said he would build a chapel in which to house them. Such a project had been at the back of his mind for a while. Initially only intended to be a gallery for the paintings, before long the chapel became a venue for weddings, naming ceremonies, parties and other events. Tim also organizes regular concerts, mostly classical, the profits of which go to charity. Visitors can still view the paintings of course, as well as admire Patricia's lovely garden and art studio. Tim sells his wine at his 'individual' cellar door in what he believes to be Margaret River's smallest winery. Eight of Tim's naïve oil paintings illustrating the traditional winemaking method are hung in the tasting room, and have recently been published as a booklet.

the next few years commuting from Narrogin and building their mud-brick home.

On Tim's retirement in 1994, they moved in, with plans to run North Devon cattle on the property. However, early one morning, after sharing a lovely bottle of local Cabernet Merlot the previous evening, Tim thought 'Why not put in a few grape vines and try making my own red wine?' What did Tim know about making wine? Well, 26 years with the Department of Agriculture hadn't been of much help! To this day, he reckons that his winemaking procedure is based on a slim booklet: 'Making Wine in Small Quantities' by Peter Gherardi, but he did also take a TAFE course in Vineyard Operations taught by Greg Bettenay, and had many a long discussion with other local

Wine tasting at Swallows Welcome
with Tim Negus and the Red Hat Ladies from Busselton

THE GROVE VINEYARD

Established: 1995

Oh dear! What's in the lake? Better not dangle your toes in the water …

Actually, it's quite safe really; you shouldn't find any crocodiles, outside zoos, this side of the Kimberleys, unless the climate warms up very quickly. The Margaret River region is,

however, home to some wonderful wildlife, including a large 'goanna' type lizard, the Southern Heath Monitor that can grow up to 1.5 metres from nose to tail tip. Unlike crocodiles, these are quite harmless so, if you are lucky enough to see one, please let it cross the road safely in front of you.

Steve of The Grove (not Irwin) has collected quite a float* of crocodiles ever since he was given one as a joke to put in his dam. He thinks it's good to have a replacement or two handy, just in case one goes walkabout. They guard a valuable little cellar door that offers, as well as its wines, a colourful array of luscious liqueurs mostly manufactured from locally sourced fruit and nuts. Lemoncello, for example, came about when Steve and Val were given a bag of lemons by a neighbour, and they didn't know what to do with them. Currently, the macadamia liqueur is a best seller. Sparkling wines are also a speciality of this winery, and spirits will soon be distilled on site, as the winery has just acquired an exciting addition in the form of a whiskey still, imported specially from Germany.

No wonder the little men are dancing! They represent The Grove Vineyard family: Steve, Val, their daughter, Rebecca, and son, Nik. They have been taken from the 'Dancingmen' font, which originated as the secret cipher used by a gang of criminals in one of Sir Arthur Conan Doyle's Sherlock Holmes adventures. Each little man substitutes for a letter of the alphabet. Can you find all of the family amongst the lily pads?

*A collective noun that means a group of crocodiles. Other words that have also been used to describe multiple crocs include a 'bask', a 'nest' and a 'congregation'. We think that a 'snap' of crocodiles might also be appropriate.

VASSE FELIX

Established: 1967

One of the challenges encountered by vignerons in the newly established Margaret River Wine Region was the problem of the birds, notably the silvereyes. In late summer, when the grapes are ripening, these small birds would naturally be feeding on the flowers of Marri trees (*Corymbia calophylla*), and fruits of plants such as the Berry Saltbush (*Rhagodia baccata*). Juicy young grapes, however, were soon discovered to be a tasty treat, and were an especially handy food source when planted near to the shelter of native forest in which the birds could hide.

A scientific study into the habits of silvereyes was commissioned, and the vignerons attempted various strategies to combat the ravages of the birds. Alternative food sources such as sunflowers were tried, and scare devices such as irregularly fired shotgun blanks or piercing whistles were used. One day at Vasse Felix, a Peregrine Falcon was found tangled in some fencing. After its rescue, farm manager, Murray Neave, built a 'hawk house' hoping that the grateful bird would stay around to dissuade the silvereyes, but unfortunately, the falcon had other ideas and disappeared, never to be seen again. Eventually, netting the vines, though costly, proved to be the most effective protection against bird damage. However, the memory of a great idea lives on in the Peregrine Falcon displayed on the Vasse Felix logo. Peregrines were threatened with extinction a few decades ago due to the widespread use

of pesticides in the 1950s and 60s. They were also disliked and often shot by pigeon fanciers, due to their habit of preying on carrier pigeons. Though still seen as a pest by some, these magnificent birds are nowadays protected worldwide, and are making a comeback.

The name of Vasse Felix commemorates a story from the region's history, with a twist. The Vasse River that flows into Geographe Bay was named after Thomas Timothée Vasse, a sailor on one of French explorer Nicholas Baudin's ships, the Naturaliste. He was swept away during a storm in the Bay in 1801, and was known thereafter as 'Unhappy Vasse'. It is a mystery to this day whether he had drowned or had survived after being washed ashore. With a feeling for the area's history, a passion for Latin, and great hopes for his new vineyard, Dr. Tom Cullity called it Vasse Felix, 'Lucky Vasse', when he planted his first vines in 1967.

Vasse Felix was the first commercial vineyard to be established in the Margaret River region. Dr. Tom Cullity's tenacity and solitary struggle during the early years of the vineyard are legendary. At the time, most people thought he was crazy to put so much effort into such an untested venture, but he kept faith with Dr. John Gladstone's vision of Margaret River's potential as a great wine growing area. The first vintage of four-year old Riesling vines was a disaster, after the fruit was largely destroyed by bunch rot and silvereyes. After all

Peregrine Falcon with
Jarrah flowers and nuts

P.Negus

the hard work, it was very depressing. The second vintage in 1972 however, won a Gold Medal in the WA Small Winemakers class and a Silver in the Open class of the Perth Show. Margaret River's worth was proven, and a grand celebration was organized. The wine flowed freely, and by all accounts it was a very good party indeed!*

Vasse Felix has been owned and operated by the Holmes a'Court family since 1987, and now includes a spacious art gallery as well as the winery and restaurant. This also serves as a venue for functions, plays and concerts, including the popular Australian Chamber Orchestra Festival that is held in early December each year. A more recent addition is a delightful sculpture walk, with artworks placed along either side of the Wilyabrup Brook that meanders through the gardens.

*In recognition of this first pioneer of the Margaret River wine industry the road south of Vasse Felix is now known as Tom Cullity Drive

Silvereyes plundering
chardonnay grapes

VOYAGER ESTATE

Established: 1991

The very first vines to be planted in Western Australia, by the first white settlers in 1829, came from South Africa. This was one reason why Voyager's owner, Michael Wright, chose South Africa's Cape Dutch style of architecture for his winery, characterised by white-rendered finishes, gracious curves and elegant gables. Having travelled to South Africa many times, he was also well aware of the striking similarities between our two countries, and decided that this style would fit well into the South West Australian landscape.

The Voyager Estate cellar door and restaurant is a magnificently elegant building with no expense spared in its construction and decoration. The warm colours and soft furnishings of the interior invite visitors to linger, relax and enjoy. Nor has there been any corner cutting with the gardens that are maintained by a team of six gardeners. The gardens serve as a grand entrance to the building, but are also a delightful place to stroll, or just to sit in quiet contemplation. The formal entrance way with its tight formation of trimmed hedges, flower beds, trees and paths is known in South Africa as a 'werf' garden. This type of garden was found in the Cape farmsteads, and was functional, being used to pen animals, grow vegetables and herbs, or even to form part of a defensive layout to discourage intruders.

Voyager Estate is well known for its roses, and the stunning gardens include many magnificent walkways featuring arches of climbing white roses. While the roses at Voyager Estate are purely aesthetic, the tradition of planting roses at the end of vine rows originally had a functional purpose as well. In the past they have been used as a first indicator of disease that may go on to affect the vines. Red roses, Satchmo, are planted with rows of red grapes, while white roses, Iceberg, are planted with the white grapes.

White roses were traditionally associated with Cape Dutch architecture, and so were an easy choice for the Voyager Estate logo. Voyager also uses the VOC logo that the Wright family acquired in 1995. This was the trademark of the Dutch East India Company, the Vereenigde Oost-Indische Compagnie, that had a monopoly on trade and navigation in all parts of the world east of the Cape of Good Hope throughout the 17th and 18th centuries. The VOC ship, the Duyfken, captained by Willem Janzsoon, made the first European landing on Australian soil at Cape York in 1606, and the Dutch were the first Europeans to explore Australia's south west coast. This often happened inadvertently, as their ships were sometimes blown too far south when travelling to their colonies in the Dutch East Indies, now Indonesia.

The VOC logo can be seen on the directional signs as you approach Voyager Estate. Finding the winery is easy though – you only have to look for the huge flag flying high over the entrance. Michael Wright wanted to show his patriotism in style, and the Voyager Estate flag is thought to be the third largest in Australia.

Iceberg

Satchmo

Europeana

Iceberg rose arches

Love Potion

WATERSHED PREMIUM WINES

Established: 2001

Watershed Premium Wines is aptly named. It is located just a short distance south of the watershed of the Margaret River, that flows west to the Indian Ocean, and 3 km north of the Chapman Brook branch of the Blackwood River, which empties into the Southern Ocean at Augusta. These two river systems are the largest in the Capes region, the Margaret being some 60 km in length, while the Blackwood is a much longer 330 km. This is by far the longest river system in the South West, and rises far out in the eastern wheatbelt near Lake Grace. The two branches of the Margaret rise in jarrah-marri forest that stretches inland from the town towards Nannup. It is fed largely by groundwater from the Leederville Aquifer that lies not far below the surface.

Squeezed between these two major river basins is Boodjidup Brook. It is just 20 km long and has a much smaller catchment. Like the Margaret, it flows westward to the Indian Ocean. Watershed overlooks this broad valley, with lovely views from the cellar door and restaurant across the vineyard. A fascinating piece of history here is that the Boodjidup Brook has yielded gold in the past, albeit in very small quantities. The first discovery was in 1896, and though there was much excitement and a small rush of claims, nothing ever came of it. A second wave of small gold discoveries came in the mid 1930s, but by then the area was cleared for dairy farming as part of the South West's Group Settlement scheme. Anxious that the scheme would be compromised by a gold rush, the government

rejected several mining claims. Settlers were threatened with the confiscation of their properties if they mined land that the government believed was more suited to agriculture.

Watershed is in good company, with Swallows Welcome, Voyager, Leeuwin and Redgate wineries all sharing the waters of Boodjidup Brook and its tributaries. Water is perhaps the most precious resource for the region's vineyards, as it is for the community as a whole. The area's abundant winter rainfall, coupled with warm, dry summers, and moderated by cooling winds from the ocean, make it ideal for the growing of grapes. This climate is very similar to that of the renowned Bordeaux wine region in France.

Watershed is one of the area's newer, larger wineries, with a carefully designed, contemporary building featuring local materials, including granite, that has been uniquely constructed to convey the appearance of a 'dry stone wall'. Apart from its literal meaning, 'Watershed' can also be interpreted to mean: " to go to a new (higher) level of understanding; an awakening" and this is the goal to which Watershed Premium Wines aspires. But CEO, Geoff Barrett, is as passionate about truffles as he is about Watershed Premium Wines. Geoff is Chairman of the Oak Valley Truffle Project that is based in Manjimup. With 75 hectares planted to Oak and Hazel trees this is the largest truffle plantation in the southern hemisphere. In the truffle season, June to August, Watershed Restaurant has several superb truffle dishes featured on its menu.

Manjimup Black Truffle

Watershed uses Manjimup black truffles in several recipes.
This one consists of:

Seared Abrolhos Scallops
Truffle Crème Brule
Crushed and roasted Hazelnuts
Manjimup Black Truffles
Watercress garnish
Recommended with Sauvignon Blanc Semillon

WILLESPIE

Established: 1976

It is not surprising that the Willespie wine label is a vibrant painting, 'Impressions of the Willespie Jewel' by Fremantle artist Henryk Szydlowski. Marian Squance, who chose the piece jointly with husband, Kevin, and their graphic designer, has a background in art teaching. The winery's name is derived from 'Wilyabrup' and the French verb *esperer*, 'to hope'. Both Marian and Kevin spent the first part of their careers teaching at primary schools all over Western Australia, from Katanning and Broomehill in the wheatbelt, to a mission school at Tincurrin, followed by an idyllic spell in the Cocos Islands, where four year old Trish wandered in & out of the classroom, & baby Jen slept in the store room! From here they moved to Watheroo, Brunswick Junction, and finally to Margaret River. The resourcefulness they developed in these years was to serve them well in their future endeavour.

It was while commuting to Brunswick from Dunsborough, that the Squances felt the pull of the land and began looking for a block on which to start their 'hobby farm'. Both had always enjoyed growing things and were looking for a change

in direction. More immediately, Trish was now owner of a beloved horse that desperately needed a more suitable home than the small paddock next door to their Dunsborough house! The block on Harmans Mill Road had all the right attributes, including a winter creek. It had originally been owned by the Harmans Mill and, fittingly, was where this mill had kept its horses.

A hundred acres, however, was rather too large for one horse. At first the Squances farmed beef cattle, but this was the period when the pioneer vineyards of the Wilyabrup Valley were being established and it seemed too good an opportunity to pass up. So with lots of help from family and friends, the work began, first to clear the paddocks of stones, and then to plant the vines. A stone and timber home was constructed in 1981. After this, the more confident owner-builders set to work on the double-storey winery and cellar door, the lovely building that is still in use today. The cellar door now doubles as gallery for jewellery and artwork by eldest daughter, Trisha Durham, who is now well established as an artist.

Three generations of the Squance family are now involved in their vineyard and winery. Kevin and Marian and the Willespie Team strive to make their wines using traditional methods. They link their lifetime of teaching experience with their present winemaking endeavours by doing things in the 'Old School' way, in particular holding back the release of their wines until they have reached optimum drinking age. On Australia Day each year they announce a special release of one of their older wines. On occasion they hold vertical tastings that allow patrons to compare a particular wine over a number of years, with limited quantities of the older vintages being made available for sale.

Their 'hope' and dream has become reality, and Kevin and Marian feel they have been very lucky in being able to pursue their passion in life. They are mindful that one should always be careful, however, and not take luck for granted. A few years ago Kevin had rather too close an encounter with his pneumatic pruning shears, a traumatic event that resulted in the loss of his thumb. As Marian wryly comments: "Kevin has put his heart and soul and part of his body into this vineyard!"

Group Settlement School

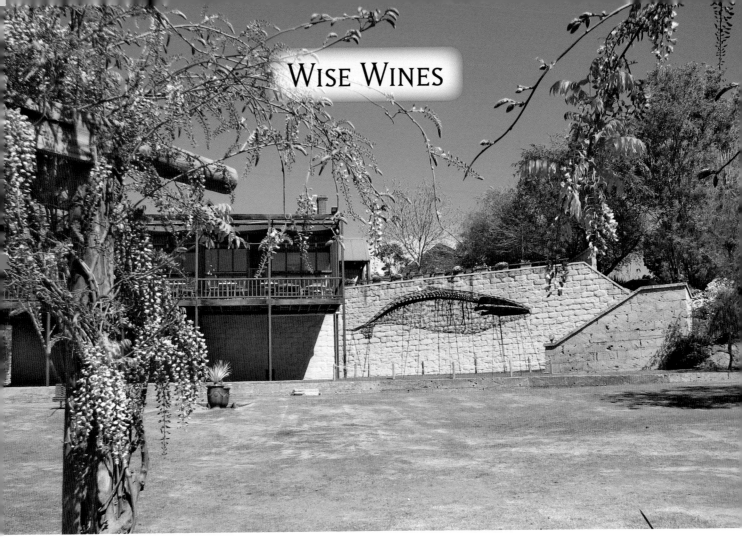

WISE WINES

Granite
Bottlebrush,
*Calothamnus
graniticus*

Established: 1983

Originally established as Geographe Bay Estate, Wise Wines came into being in 1992 when Ron and Sandra Wise combined it with the nearby Eagle Bay Estate that they had bought previously in 1986. The Eagle Bay vineyard is reduced now to plantings of Cabernet Sauvignon and Shiraz, producing the flagship Eagle Bay Wines, whilst fruit sourced from growers in Margaret River, Pemberton and Frankland River, all cool climate regions, is used in the production of the diverse range of Wises' wines. The restaurant is now leased and run as a separate enterprise.

This would have to be one of the closest vineyards to the sea in the Margaret River Wine Region, and the breathtaking view from the restaurant deck across the treetops of the Meelup Regional Park to Geographe Bay is a highlight of this winery. The Meelup Regional Park is a superb stretch of bushland running from Dunsborough to Eagle Bay that protects a diverse and very special flora, including some species that are found nowhere else in the world. Several orchids are unique to the area, and the Busselton Shire floral emblem, a subspecies of the Granite Bottlebrush that is illustrated here, occurs only here and in adjacent parts of the Leeuwin-Naturaliste National Park around Cape Naturaliste. A delightful bush

trail meanders 7 km through the Meelup Park, all or part of which makes a great stroll before wine tasting and lunch at Wise Wines!

The sea urchin motif on the Wise Wine labels also connects the winery with the ocean. The sea air does not adversely affect the grapes - on the contrary, the sea breezes are advantageous in keeping the vines cool and protecting the fruit from the mildew and botrytis that are caused by humidity. The whole of the Capes coastline between Geographe Bay and Augusta is in the process of being designated a Marine National Park, thus protecting the unique ecosystem that lies beneath the waves. If you look carefully out to sea in spring, between September and

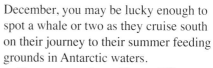

December, you may be lucky enough to spot a whale or two as they cruise south on their journey to their summer feeding grounds in Antarctic waters.

Fremantle sculptor, Simon Gilby made the two vineyard workers that you pass as you enter the property, and that are featured in our painting. He also sculpted the magnificent whale on the lawn beneath the cellar door and restaurant. The eagle is the work of another well-known West Australian artist, Len Zuks.

WOODLANDS WINES

Yellow-breasted Robins nesting in a Snottygobble

Established: 1973

After a 300 km drive from Perth, the Watson family usually arrived late in the evening at their new vineyard. The gate with 'Woodlands' worked into the metal, was a present from David's parents, and had been set back from busy Caves Road, to give safer entry to the property. The children, Stuart, Andrew and Elizabeth were always excited to see the Tawny Frogmouth owls sitting on the gate to greet them each time they turned into the driveway. With its substantial grove of Peppermint and Marri trees, Woodlands is sited on prime viticultural land and is a haven away from the city; home to possums, a wide variety of birds, and alive with the sound of a thousand frogs, always a sign of a healthy environment. David and Heather had a dream of establishing a vineyard in the Margaret River area.

During Easter 1973 David and Heather Watson were staying in Busselton when they had a small serendipitous disaster with a fire that caused their chimney to catch alight! While waiting for the smoke to clear, they took a walk and in the window of a nearby real estate agent they noticed a 20 acre block advertised for sale. They were very excited as the block was in a perfect location, in the Wilyabrup Valley, on the corner of Caves and Woodlands Roads, just across from the Metricup Road corner.

An odd condition of the sale was that the owners, Paul and Hilda Ensor so respected Paul's mother, Mrs Ensor Senior, that she had to approve the buyers, as she wanted to ensure that the precious land would be sold into good hands. Luckily, Heather and David met her, and passed the test. They were able to buy the block.

The Watson family's friendship with the Mann family of the Swan Valley fuelled David's winemaking aspirations and David was eager to bring his dream to fruition. The real test, however, was just beginning. Heather and David needed extraordinary resourcefulness and perseverance to get a vineyard started in a new area. Heather was a child of a soldier settler, Matt Burns and his wife, Ivy. Their Karridale venture sadly ended in heartache, but Ivy always talked of the whole of the South West being planted to vines, and Heather especially remembers the knowledge and help she received from her mother and family. Oldest son, Stuart, recalls in the early days going in the dark to the dam with Nanny Ivy to catch gilgies. There were many challenges including the backbreaking tasks of felling large Marri trees by hand, clearing bush, preparing the soil, planting and the long manual hours tending the vines. It was almost the last straw when they arrived late one night to find all their newly planted vines eaten and ripped up by cows from a neighbouring farm. Thousands of wet cow pads covered the soil. As the vines began to produce, the kangaroos were constant diners on the grapes. It was a huge undertaking, juggling weekend trips from Perth with the full-time careers of David as a young engineer and Heather as a student lawyer and carer of their three children, who spent many hours in their baby baskets around the vineyard.

There were many hardships but there were good times too, and firm friendships were established with neighbouring vineyard pioneers, David and Ann Greg, Dr. Tom Cullity of Vasse Felix, and Di and Kevin Cullen and their family. Stuart especially remembers the real cellar with a trapdoor at Cullens, a wonderful place for games of hide-and-seek! There were late afternoons with Kevin Cullen playing the piano and singing with the children after he and David had finished a game of tennis; and many happy hours were spent in the unlined shed, lit by Tilley Lanterns and warmed by the wood fire, with family and friends crowded in for meals and accommodation.

The hard work and perseverance was rewarded in 1982 when Woodlands' first Cabernet Sauvignon won top awards at the Perth, Mt Barker, and Canberra Wine Shows. The Watson family's dedication to quality has continued to the present day to win them international acclaim as one of the region's top wine producers. Heather likes to think of the little figure on their logo as their angel of the woods, looking after the family and their vines. The old lady's judgement on who should inherit this small, special parcel of land has certainly proven to be wise.

P. Negus

WOODY NOOK WINES

Established: 1982

Jeff and Wynn Gallagher purchased their 20 hectares at Woody Nook in 1978. Like many people lured to the South West in the 1970s, they were aiming at self-sufficiency on a small property, so they built their own mud brick home, and tried various ventures that included raising thirty Angora goats at one stage! Eventually, winemaking seemed like a good option, and their first vines were planted in 1982, with the first vintage following in 1987.

The property was formerly a sawmill and sleeper-cutters' operation. In the early days of white settlement before mechanization, sleeper cutters, many of them European migrants, felled logs from south west forests using a narrow axe, then cut and squared sleepers from the fallen timber using wedges and a broad axe. South West hardwoods, particularly Jarrah, *Eucalyptus marginata*, were ideal for railway sleepers due to their durability and resistance to insect attack. The sleepers were a valuable export commodity, but they were also in demand locally, at first for the network of railways used to transport logs to port during the thriving timber industry era of the late 19th century, and then for the railway lines that serviced the growing population centres throughout the South West. The railway line from Perth to Busselton was extended to Margaret River in 1924, passing fairly near to Woody Nook, and was completed to Flinders Bay, Augusta, in 1925. It was a lifeline to the group settlers of the area as road transport was primitive, consisting only of rutted cart tracks that were often soft and sandy in summer and thick with mud in winter.

With the advent of motor vehicles, and improvements to the roads, the railway lost momentum in the 1950s and was closed in 1957. However, the railway reserve is currently undergoing a new lease of life as a recreational walk and cycle track that is gradually being extended from Margaret River north to Busselton and south to Augusta.

You can still see remnants of the old sawmill around the car park and when Jeff and Wynn bought the farm, an old two-handled saw was still stuck in one of the trees! In 2000 Woody Nook passed to new owners, Peter and Jane Bailey, but continuity was maintained with Jeff and Wynn's son, Neil Gallagher, staying on as winemaker.

The timber-cutting days are remembered in Woody Nook's 'Killdog Creek' wine series, while the 'Kelly's Farewell' wines commemorate the pioneering Bussell family who moved from Vasse (now Busselton) to establish a farm at Ellensbrook in the 1850s. Read the stories behind the names on the bottle labels when you visit Woody Nook.

Remains of the original saw with Western Rosellas and young Magpies

XANADU WINES

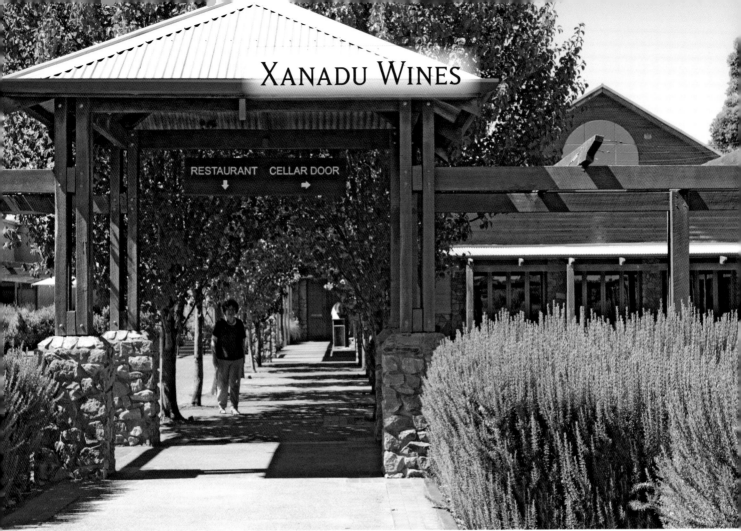

An unusual weather-vane on the road to Xanadu

Established: 1977

> *In Xanadu did Kubla Khan*
> *A stately pleasure-dome decree*
> *Where Alph, the sacred river, ran*
> *Through caverns measureless to man*
> *Down to a sunless sea*

The famous poem by Samuel Taylor Coleridge provided inspiration for the name of Dr John Lagan's new venture when he started his vineyard in 1977, only a few years after the first pioneers of the wine industry in the Margaret River region. He was a great lover of poetry and no doubt saw the "stately pleasure-dome" as a fitting description for his future winery.

John Lagan and Eithne Sheridan Lagan both came to Margaret River as doctors from Ireland in 1968, in answer to an advertisement in the British Medical Journal. They were looking for a brighter future in Australia, but instead found Margaret River to be a pretty depressed area at that time, with a declining population and the hospital in danger of closing. The region was then a rural backwater, sustained by dairying and the timber industry, neither of which were particularly prosperous. It was a long way from Perth and the only cultural facility in the town was a public library.

Initially, the Lagans took only 12 months leave from their practice in Ireland, and at first it seemed that they would be going straight back at the end of the year. By then, however, things were starting to improve, as John had set up an additional practice in Kwinana near Perth. Around this time, he met Drs. Kevin Cullen and Tom Cullity, who encouraged him to buy land for viticulture in the Margaret River area. In 1971, the Lagans bought 200 acres for $50 an acre, followed by another 200 for $65 an acre the following year. After much preparation work, Chateau Xanadu was registered in 1975 and the first vines planted in 1977. The 'Chateau', that was later dropped from the name, gave that extra hint of grandeur, in keeping with John's dream of a mighty French-style estate. Certainly, there was grandeur in the long, winding driveway through the now extensive plantings of vines, and in the spacious cellar door, function centre and restaurant that was built from granite, excavated from the property.

John Lagan was one of the colourful characters of the district, a lover of poetry and theatre. In 1985 he established 'La Grande Guild of Margaret River Vignerons', together with Bill Ullinger of Redgate Wines and Barney Blain, then owner of Rivers Bend Wines. A ceremony was held prior to the start of vintage each year that involved the donning of extravagant robes, fashioned at great expense, to proclaim the 'Declaration of Vendange'. This was done in the company of most of the district's vignerons, with great fanfare, poetry readings and the consumption and appreciation of considerable quantities of the previous year's vintage.

In 2005, Xanadu Wines was purchased the Rathbone family, after a period of corporate ownership. Darren Rathbone's vision for Xanadu Wines is a vineyard concentrating on smaller production of high quality grapes that will translate into premium quality wines, as befits one of Margaret River's oldest and best known wineries.

Stephan and Suzie, manager and vineyard manager, enjoy a glass of wine to celebrate the end of the day, as we celebrate the end of our book.

Cheers!

GRAPE VARIETIES BY VINEYARD

	Semillon	Sauvignon Blanc	Chenin Blanc	Reisling	Chardonnay	Verdelho	Vioignier	Marsanne	Cab. Sauvignon	Shiraz	Merlot	Malbec	Cabernet Franc	Tempranillo	Pinot Noir	Zinfandel	Petit Verdot
Adinfern	√	√			√				√	√	√	√			√		
Anniebrook	√	√			√					√			√	√			
Aravina	√	√	√		√		√		√	√	√						
Bettenays	√	√			√				√	√	√						
Brookland Valley	√	√			√				√	√	√						
Brookwood	√	√	√						√	√							
Brown Hill	√	√							√	√	√						
Cape Grace			√		√				√	√							
Cape Mentelle	√	√			√				√	√	√					√	
Cape Naturaliste	√	√							√	√	√						
Churchview	√	√	√	√	√	√		√	√	√	√	√				√	
Clairault Wines	√	√			√				√		√		√				√
Cullen	√	√			√				√		√	√	√		√		√
Edwards	√	√			√				√	√	√						
Firetail	√	√							√		√						
Flying Fish	√	√	√		√				√	√	√						
Gralyn	√			√	√				√	√							
Hamelin Bay	√	√			√				√	√	√						
Happs	√	√	√		√	√	√	√	√	√	√	√			√	√	√
Hay Shed	√	√			√				√	√	√		√	√			√
Heydon Estate	√	√			√		√		√	√							√
Howard Park	√				√				√	√	√		√				√
Howling Wolves	√	√	√		√				√	√	√	√					
Island Brook	√	√			√	√			√		√				√		
Knotting Hill	√	√			√	√	√		√	√	√	√	√				
Lamonts	√	√	√	√	√	√		√	√	√	√	√					
Laurance	√	√			√				√	√	√						
Leeuwin		√		√	√				√	√							
Lenton Brae	√	√			√				√		√						
Marri Wood	√	√	√						√								
McHenry Hohnen	√	√			√		√	√	√	√	√	√			√	√	√
McLeod Creek	√	√			√				√	√	√						
Minot	√	√							√								

	Semillon	Sauvignon Blanc	Chenin Blanc	Reisling	Chardonnay	Verdelho	Vioignier	Marsanne	Cab. Sauvignon	Shiraz	Merlot	Malbec	Cabernet Franc	Tempranillo	Pinot Noir	Zinfandel	Petit Verdot
Pierro	√	√			√				√		√				√		
Preveli	√	√							√		√				√		
Redgate	√	√	√		√				√	√	√		√				
Rosily	√	√			√				√	√							
Saracen	√	√			√				√	√							
Swallows									√		√		√				
The Grove	√	√			√	√			√	√	√			√	√		
Vasse Felix	√	√			√				√	√	√						
Voyager	√	√	√		√				√	√	√						
Watershed	√	√			√		√		√	√	√		√			√	
Willespie	√	√		√	√	√			√	√	√		√				
Wise Wines	√	√		√	√	√	√		√	√	√				√		√
Woodlands					√				√		√	√	√		√		√
Woody Nook	√	√	√		√				√	√	√		√	√			
Xanadu	√	√			√				√								

Other varieties:

Churchview: Grenache, Mouvedre

Flying Fish Cove: Sangiovese

Happs Karridale Planting: Reds: Merlot, Cabernet Sauvignon, Tempranillo, Shiraz, Pinot Noir, Muscat, Tinta Cao, Cabernet Franc, Graciano, Malbec, Gamay, Bastado, Nebbiolo, Sangiovese, Carignan, Mourvedre, Grenache, Petit Verdot, Cinsaut; Whites: Semillon, Chardonnay, Sauvignon Blanc, Viognier, Verdelho, Chenin, Furmint, Marsanne, Muscadelle

Happs Dunsborough Vineyard: Reds: Cabernet Sauvignon, Shiraz, Merlot, Touriga, Tinta Cao, Souzao, Muscat; Whites: Chardonnay, Verdelho

Hay Shed Hill: Muscat

Howard Park: Muscat

Island Brook: Sangiovese

McHenry Hohnen: Rousanne, Grenache, Graciano, Mataro

The Grove Vineyard: Graciano

Watershed: Sangiovese

Woody Nook: Graciano

Wine Styles By Vineyard

	Dry Whites	Dry Reds	Rosé	Sweet Wines	Sparkling	Fortified	Liqueurs
Adinfern	√	√		√	√	√	
Anniebrook	√	√	√	√		√	
Aravina	√	√					
Berry Farm	√			√	√	√	√
Bettenays	√	√	√	√		√	
Blackwood Meadery	√			√			√
Brookland Valley	√	√	√				
Brookwood	√	√	√	√			
Brown Hill	√	√	√	√			
Cape Grace	√	√		√			
Cape Mentelle	√	√					
Cape Naturaliste	√	√					
Churchview	√	√	√			√	
Clairault Wines	√	√	√	√		√	
Cullen	√	√			√		
Edwards	√	√					
Firetail	√	√	√				
Flying Fish Cove	√	√	√		√	√	
Gralyn	√	√	√	√		√	
Hamelin Bay	√	√	√				
Happs	√	√	√	√		√	
Hay Shed Hill	√	√	√	√			
Heydon Estate	√	√		√			
Howard Park	√	√	√		√		
Howling Wolves	√	√	√	√	√		
Island Brook	√	√		√			
Knotting Hill	√	√		√			
Lamonts	√	√	√	√	√	√	√
Laurance	√	√	√	√			
Leeuwin	√	√			√		

	Dry Whites	Dry Reds	Rosé	Sweet Wines	Sparkling	Fortified	Liqueurs
Lenton Brae	√	√		√			
Marri Wood Park	√	√			√		
McHenry Hohnen	√	√					
McLeod Creek	√	√					
Minot	√	√					
Pierro	√	√					
Preveli	√	√			√		
Redgate	√	√	√	√		√	
Rosily	√	√					
Saracen	√	√	√				
Swallows Welcome		√	√			√	
The Grove	√	√		√	√	√	√
Vasse Felix	√	√		√	√		
Voyager	√	√		√	√		
Watershed	√	√	√	√	√		
Willespie	√	√			√	√	
Wise Wines	√	√	√	√	√	√	
Woodlands	√	√					
Woody Nook	√	√	√	√		√	
Xanadu	√	√	√	√		√	

Other styles:

Happs: Preservative Free range
Berry Farm: Fruit Wines
Blackwood Meadery: Honey Wines

Facilities

	Restaurant	Café	Gallery	Playground[†]
Adinfern Estate				
Anniebrook				
Aravina	√	√	√	√
Berry Farm		√		
Bettenays				
Blackwood Meadery				
Brookland Valley	√		√	
Brookwood Estate		√		
Brown Hill				
Cape Grace				
Cape Mentelle		√		√
Cape Naturaliste				
Churchview				
Clairault Winest	√			
Cullen Wines	√			
Edwards Wines				
Firetail Wines				
Flying Fish				
Gralyn Wines				
Hamelin Bay Wines		√		
Happs			√	
Hay Shed Hill		√	√	
Heydon Estate				
Howard Park				
Howling Wolves				
Island Brook Estate				

	Restaurant	Café	Gallery	Playground[†]
Knotting Hill		√		
Lamonts	√		√	
Laurance Wines	√		√	√
Leeuwin Estate	√		√	
Lenton Brae				
Marri Wood Park		√		
McHenry Hohnen		√		
McLeod Creek				
Minot Wines				
Pierro				
Preveli Wines				
Redgate				
Rosily				
Saracen Estates	√		√	√
Swallows Welcome				√
The Grove Vineyard		√		
Vasse Felix	√		√	
Voyager Estate	√		√	
Watershed	√	√		√
Willespie			√	
Wise Wines	√			
Woodlands				
Woody Nook	√			√
Xanadu Wines	√			√

Café: light meals/platters only
† Playground: dedicated playground equipment

CONTACTS

1 The GPS coordinates in the contact details are for the entrance to the winery driveway or driveways, not for the winery building.

2 Opening days and times vary considerably, so do telephone the winery ahead of time to ensure that they will be open when you plan to visit.

3 Check the *Downloads, Updates and Corrections* page on http://www.capetocape.8m.com for changes and corrections in these contact details. If you find contact information that is changed or wrong please let us know at capetocape@smartchat.net.au.

Adinfern Estate
Address: 8772 Bussell Hwy, Cowaramup 6284
    Postal: PO Box 249, Cowaramup 6284
33° 53.03'S   115°05.28'E
Tel: +61 8 9755 5272   Fax: +61 8 9755 5206
E-mail: wine@adinfern.com
Website: www.adinfern.com

Anniebrook
Address: 247 Wildwood Road, Carbunup 6280
33°41.83'S   115° 09.83'E
Tel: +61 8 9755 1155   Fax: +61 8 9755 1138
E-mail: info@anniebrook.com.au
Website: www.anniebrookwineandflowers.com.au

Aravina Estate
Address: 61 Thornton Road, Yallingup
    Postal: PO Box 563, Dunsborough 6281
33° 42.06'S   115° 04.65'E
Tel: +61 8 9750 1111   Fax: +61 8 9750 1155
E-mail: info@aravinaestate.com
Website: www.aravinaestate.com

Berry Farm
Address: 43 Bessell Rd, Rosa Glen 6285
34° 00.38'S   115° 12.28'E
Tel: +61 8 9757 5054   Fax: +61 8 9757 5116
E-mail: info@berryfarm.com.au
Website: www.berryfarm.com.au

Bettenay Wines
Address: 594 Miamup Road, Wilyabrup or 248 Tom Cullity Drive, Wilyabrup
    Postal: PO Box 329, Cowaramup 6284
33° 48.91'S   115° 03.60'E (Tom Cullity Drive entry)
33° 49.21'S   115° 03.66'E (Miamup Road entry)
Tel: +61 8 97 555 539   Mob: +61 8 419 838 435
E-mail: info@bettenaywines.com.au
Website: www.bettenaysmargaretriver.com.au

Blackwood Meadery
Address: 764 Brockman Hwy, Karridale 6288
34° 10.51'S   115° 10.42'E
Tel/Fax: +61 8 9758 2332
E-mail: blackwoodmeadery@gmail.com
Web Page: www.margaretriver.com/accom_result1/blackwood-meadery

Brookland Valley
Address: 4070 Caves Road, Wilyabrup
    Postal: PO Box 180, Cowaramup 6284
33° 47.85'S   115° 01.78'E
Tel: +61 8 9755 6042   Fax: +61 8 9755 6214
E-mail: cellar@brooklandvalley.com.au
Website: www.brooklandvalley.com.au

Brookwood Estate
Address: 430 Treeton Road, Cowaramup 6284
    Postal: PO Box 247, Cowaramup 6284
33° 50.90'S   115° 08.93'E
Tel: +61 8 9755 5604   Fax: +61 8 9755 5870
E-mail: cellardoorsales@brookwood.com.au
Website: www.brookwood.com.au

Brown Hill Estate
Address: 925 Rosa Brook Road (cnr. Barrett Road), Rosa Brook
    Postal: RMB 319, Rosa Brook 6285
33° 57.24'S   115° 10.28'E
Tel: +61 8 9757 4003   Fax: +61 8 9757 4004   Free call: 1800 185 044
E-mail: cellardoor@brownhillestate.com.au
Website: www.brownhillestate.com.au

Cape Grace Wines
Address: 281 Fifty One Road, Cowaramup
    Postal: PO Box 325, Cowaramup 6284
33° 50.71'S   115° 03.21'E
Tel: +61 8 9755 5669   Fax: +61 8 9755 5668
E-mail: info@capegracewines.com.au
Website: www.capegracewines.com.au

Cape Mentelle
Address: 331 Wallcliffe Road, Margaret River
    Postal: PO Box 110, Margaret River 6285
33° 57.56'S   115° 02.32'E
Tel: +61 8 9757 0888   Fax: +61 8 9757 3233
E-mail: info@capementelle.com.au
Website: www.capementelle.com.au

Cape Naturaliste Vineyard
Address: 1 Coley Road (off Caves Road), Yallingup 6282
33° 39.94'S   115° 01.87'E
Tel/Fax: +61 8 9755 2538
E-mail: capenat@iinet.net.au
Website: www.capenaturalistevineyard.com.au

Churchview Estate
Address: 8 Gale Road (cnr. Bussell Hwy), Metricup 6280
33° 46.73'S   115° 08.00'E
Tel: +61 8 9755 7200   Fax: +61 8 9755 7300
E-mail: info@churchview.com.au
Website: www.churchview.com.au

Clairault Wines
Address: 3277 Caves Rd, Wilyabrup or Henry Road, Wilyabrup
    Postal: PO Box 360, Dunsborough 6281
33° 43.74'S   115° 02.28'E (Caves Road entry)
33° 44.17'S   115° 04.21'E (Henry Road entry)
Tel: +61 8 9755 6655   Fax: +61 8 9755 6229
E-mail: clairault@clairaultwines.com.au
Website: www.clairaultwines.com.au

Cullen Wines
Address: 4323 Caves Road, Wilyabrup
    Postal: PO Box 17, Cowaramup 6284
33° 49.15'S   115° 02.21'E
Tel: +61 8 9755 5277   Fax: +61 8 9755 5550
E-mail: enquiries@cullenwines.com.au
Website: www.cullenwines.com.au

Edwards Wines
Address: 687 Ellen Brook Road (cnr. Caves road), Cowaramup 6284
33° 53.77'S   115° 01.70'E
Tel: +61 8 9755 5999   Fax: +61 8 9755 5988
E-mail: info@edwardswines.com.au
Website: www.edwardswines.com.au

Firetail Wines
Address: 21 Bessell Road, Rosa Glen
   Postal: Roje Estates, PO Box 791, Margaret River 6285
34° 00.34'S   115° 12.15'E
Tel: +61 8 9757 5156   Fax: +61 8 9757 5156
E-mail: wines@firetail.com.au
Website: www.firetail.com.au

Flying Fish Cove
Address: 3763 Caves Road, Wilyabrup
   Postal: PO Box 692, Dunsborough 6281
33° 46.23'S   115° 02.05'E
Tel: +61 8 9755 6600   Fax: +61 8 9755 6788
E-mail: cellardoor@flyingfishcove.com
Website: www.flyingfishcove.com

Gralyn Estate
Address: 4145 Caves Road, Wilyabrup
   Postal: c/- PO, Cowaramup 6284
33° 48.25'S   115° 01.87'E
Tel: +61 8 9755 6245   Fax: +61 8 9755 6136
E-mail: info@gralyn.com.au
Website: www.gralyn.com.au

Hamelin Bay Wines
Address: 199 McDonald Road, Karridale 6288
34° 10.47'S   115°07.12'E
Tel/Fax: +61 8 9758 6779
E-mail: info@hbwines.com.au
Website: www.hbwines.com.au

Happs Vineyard & Pottery
Address: 575 Commonage Road, Dunsborough 6281
33° 39.92'S   115°05.65'E
Tel: 61 8 9755 3300   Fax: 61 8 9755 3846
E-mail: happs@happs.com.au
Website: www.happs.com.au
Pottery Tel: +61 8 9755 3479   Fax: +61 8 9755 3846
E-mail: jacquie@happspottery.com.au
Website: www.happspottery.com.au

Hay Shed Hill
Address: 511 Harmans Mill Road, Wilyabrup
   Postal: PO Box 221, Cowaramup 6284
33° 47.73'S   115° 04.08'E
Tel: +61 8 9755 6046   Fax: +61 8 9755 6083
E-mail: info@hayshedhill.com.au
Website: www.hayshedhill.com.au

Heydon Estate
Address: 325 Tom Cullity Drive, Wilyabrup
   Postal: c/o Post Office, Cowaramup 6284
33° 48.58'S   115° 03.90'E
Tel: +61 8 9755 6995   Fax: +61 8 9755 6996
E-mail: info@heydonestate.com.au
Website: www.heydonestate.com.au

Howard Park Wines
Address: 543 Miamup Road, Cowaramup or cnr Brockman and Fifty
   One Road, Cowaramup
   Postal: PO Box 283, Cowaramup 6284
33° 49.34'S   115° 03.89'E (Miamup Road entry)
33° 49.96'S   115° 03.14'E (Brockman Road entry)
Tel: +61 8 9756 5200   Fax: +61 8 9756 5222
E-mail: margaretriver@hpw.com.au
Website: www.howardparkwines.com.au

Howling Wolves
Address: 5 Harmans Mill Road, Metricup 6280 (cnr Bussell Hwy)
33° 48.28'S   115° 07.25'E
Tel: +61 8 9755 7409   Fax: +61 8 9755 7400
E-mail: winery@howlingwolveswines.com
Website: www.howlingwolveswines.com

Island Brook Estate
Address: 7388 Bussell Highway, Metricup 6280
33° 45.22'S   115° 09.26'E
Tel: +61 8 9755 7501   Fax: +61 8 9755 7178
E-mail: islandbrook@bigpond.com
Website: www.islandbrook.com.au

Knotting Hill Estate
Address: 247 Carter Road, Wilyabrup 6280
33° 46.71'S   115° 05.32'E
Tel: +61 8 9755 7733   Fax: +61 8 9755 7744
E-mail: admin@knottinghill.com.au
Website: www.knottinghill.com.au

Lamonts, Margaret River
Address: 96 Koorabin Drive (Cnr. Gunyulgup Valley Road),
   Yallingup 6282
33° 40.00'S   115° 02.72'E
Tel: +61 8 9755 2434   Fax: +61 8 9755 2435
E-mail: margaretriver@lamonts.com.au
Website: www.lamonts.com.au

Laurance Wines
Address: 3478 Caves Road, Wilyabrup 6280
33° 44.75'S   115° 01.80'E
Tel: +61 8 9750 4000   Fax: +61 8 9750 4004
E-mail: info@laurancewines.com
Website: www.laurancewines.com

Leeuwin Estate
Address: 157 Stevens Road, Margaret River 6285
34° 00.42'S   115° 03.09'E
Tel: +61 8 9759 0000   Fax: +61 8 9759 0001
E-mail: info@leeuwinestate.com.au
Website: www.leeuwinestate.com.au

Lenton Brae Estate
Address: 3887 Caves Road, Wilyabrup
   Postal: PO Box 500 Margaret River 6285
33° 46.90'S   115° 02.02'E
Tel: +61 8 97556255   Fax: +61 8 9755 6268
E-mail: info@lentonbrae.com
Website: www.lentonbrae.com

Marri Wood Park
Address: 28 Whittle Road (off Caves Road), Yallingup 6282
33° 40.90'S   115° 01.68'E
Tel/Fax: +61 8 9755 2343   Mob: +61 4 0354 7734
E-mail: query@marriwoodpark.com.au
Website: www.marriwoodpark.com.au

McHenry Hohnen Vintners
Address: 5962 Caves Road, Margaret River
   Postal: PO Box 1480, Margaret River 6285
33° 57.21'S   115° 00.86'E
Tel: +61 8 9757 9684   Fax: +61 8 9757 9176
E-mail: info@mchv.com.au
Website: www.mchv.com.au

McLeod Creek Wines
Address: 10 McLeod Creek Road, Karridale 6288
34°09.71'S   115°05.96'E
Tel: +61 8 9758 5020   Fax: +61 8 9758 5145
E-mail: info@mcleodcreekwines.com.au
Website: www.mcleodcreekwines.com.au

Minot Wines
Address: 26 Harrington Road, Margaret River
   Postal: PO Box 683, Margaret River 6285
33° 59.07'S   115° 02.52'E
Tel: +61 8 9757 3579   Fax: +61 8 9757 2361
E-mail: minot@wn.com.au
Website: www.minotwines.com.au

Pierro
Address: 4051 Caves Road, Wilyabrup
    Postal: PO Box 522, Busselton 6280
33° 47.75'S   115° 01.82'E
Tel: +61 8 97556220   Fax: +61 8 9755 6308
E-mail: info@pierro.com.au
Web: www.pierro.com.au

Preveli Wines
Address: Prevelly Liquor Store, 99 Mitchell Drive, Prevelly 6285
    Postal: PO Box 18, Margaret River 6285
33° 58.72'S   114° 59.65'E
Tel: +61 8 9757 2374   Fax: +61 8 9757 2790
E-mail: preveli@preveliwines.com.au
Website: www.preveliwines.com.au

Redgate Wines
Address: 659 Boodjidup Road, Margaret River
    Postal: PO Box 117, Margaret River 6285
34° 00.46'S   115° 02.15'E
Tel: +61 8 9757 6488   Fax: +61 8 9757 6308
E-mail: info@redgatewines.com.au
Website: www.redgatewines.com.au

Rosily Vineyard
Address: 871 Yelverton Road, Wilyabrup 6280.
33° 45.78'S   115° 04.71'E
Tel: +61 8 9755 6336   Fax: +61 8 9755 6336
E-mail: sam@rosily.com.au
Website: www.rosily.com.au

Saracen Estates
Address: 3517 Caves Road, Wilyabrup 6280
33° 44.94'S   115° 01.76'E
Tel: +61 8 9755 6099 (Cellar Door)   Fax: +61 8 9755 6011
E-mail: sales@saracenestates.com.au
Website: www.saracenestates.com.au

Swallows Welcome
Address: 542 Wallis Road, Witchcliffe
    Postal: PO Box 771, Margaret River 6285
34° 00.15'S   115° 07.10'E
Tel/Fax: +61 8 9757 6348
E-mail: swallowswelcome@bigpond.com

The Grove Vineyard
Address: 213 Carter Road, Wilyabrup 6280
33° 46.89'S   115° 05.38'E
Tel: +61 8 9755 7458
E-mail: info@thegrovevineyard.com.au
Website: www.thegrovevineyard.com.au

Vasse Felix
Address: 4357 Caves Road, Cowaramup
    Postal: PO Box 32, Cowaramup 6284
33° 49.35'S   115° 02.24'E
Tel: +61 8 9756 5000   Fax: +61 8 9755 5424
E-mail: info@vassefelix.com.au
Website: www.vassefelix.com.au

Voyager Estate
Address: 41 Stevens Road, Margaret River 6285
33° 59.78'S   115° 03.09'E
Tel: +61 8 9757 6354   Fax: +61 8 9757 6494
E-mail: wineroom@voyagerestate.com.au
Website: voyagerestate.com.au

Watershed Premium Wines
Address: 6 Darch Road (cnr. Bussell Highway), Margaret River
    Postal: PO Box 893, Margaret River 6285
33° 59.53'S   115° 05.45'E
Tel: +61 8 9758 8633   Fax: +61 8 9757 3999
E-mail: cellar@watershedwines.com.au
Website: www.watershedwines.com.au

Willespie
Address: 555 Harmans Mill Road, Wilyabrup 6280
33° 47.55'S   115° 03.95'E
Tel: +61 8 9755 6248   Fax: +61 8 9755 6210
E-mail: willespie@bigpond.com.au
Website: www.willespie.com.au

Wise Wines
Address: 80 Eagle Bay Road, Eagle Bay 6281
33° 34.81'S   115° 04.00'E
Tel: +61 8 9750 3100
E-mail: cellar@wisewine.com.au
Website: www.wisewine.com.au

Woodlands Wines
Address: 3948 Caves Road Wilyabrup
    Postal: PO Box 220 Cowaramup 6284
33° 47.22'S   115° 02.00'E
Tel: +61 8 9755 6226   Fax: +61 8 9755 6236
E-mail: mail@woodlandswines.com
Website: www.woodlandswines.com

Woody Nook Wines
Address: 506 Metricup Road, Wilyabrup 6280
33° 46.91'S   115° 04.83'E
Tel: +61 8 9755 7547   Fax: +61 8 9755 7007
E-mail: info@woodynook.com.au
Website: www.woodynook.com.au

Xanadu Wines
Address: 316 Boodjidup Road, Margaret River
    Postal: PO Box 144, Margaret River 6285
33° 58.96'S   115° 03.39'E
Tel: +61 8 9758 9500   Fax: +61 8 9757 3389
E-mail: info@xanaduwines.com
Website: www.xanaduwines.com

Bibliography

Cresswell, Gail J. *The Light of Leeuwin: the Augusta-Margaret River Shire History*. AMR Shire History Group, 1989

Cullity, Garrett J. *Vasse Felix: the early years of wine in Margaret River, 1966 – 1973*. 2010

Edwards, Brian *The Matilda Mission*. Coolindah, 1993

Edwards, Geoffrey *The Road to Prevelly*. 1989

Marchant, Leslie R. *France Australe*. Scott Four Colour Print, 1998

Marchant, Leslie R. *French Napoleonic Placenames of the South West Coast*. RIC Publications, 2004

Terry, Frances *They Came to the Margaret*. 2nd. Reprint, 1988

Wenman, Tom *There's Gold in Margaret River*. 2006

Zekulich, Michael *Wine Western Australia*. St. George Books, 1994